From
Brexit
to
Bregret

Dedication

This book is dedicated to the people suffering from Brexit.

.

From Brexit
To Bregret

Thomas Klikauer

https://klikauer.wordpress.com

KDP

Preface

This book is a collection of eight articles that were all published online on various news websites during the years of the political discussions of the United Kingdom (UK) exiting the European Union (EU) – 2016 to 2023. This became known as Brexit. The period of Brexit also included negotiations between the UK and the EU. Brexit – more or less – began, at least semi-officially, when the then conservative prime minister David Cameron issued an election promise to leave the EU – on 23rd January 2013.

All chapters were published in the USA and India between 2016 and 2023. The content remains original and un-altered as published during the Brexit years. Besides these, the book also includes two newly added chapters: an introduction outlining the purpose and structure of the book and a conclusion that addresses the question, *what can we learn from this book?*

Books are always a combined effort – a book almost all the time needs more than one person. As a consequence, I would like to thank, first of all, my original proof-readers: Catherine Link, Gyoergy Szell, and Meg Young.

Yet, my foremost thanks go to Meg Young, who not only did the initial grouping of articles but also the final proofreading of the entire book, and for submitting the book to https://kdp.amazon.com. Without Meg's assiduous editorial work, battle with the author's grammar, and hours of dedication in converting German-English into English-English, this book would have never been possible.

Secondly, I would like to thank Ralf Itzwerth for IT support and Chris Young for his amazing job on the book cover, and Danny Antonelli for his great insight on KDP publishing, website issues, the main marketplace, pricing, and marketing.

The second thanks go to three women: my boss (Louise); my co-supervisor for PhDs (Nadine); and my co-lecturer of a master class we teach together (Catherine). All three kept the sheer endless amount of university admin away from me – as much as possible.

The seemingly ever-increasing amount of administrative work is put onto academics by university managers creating *academentia* – the inability to function as an academic. Largely freed from this, I was able to complete this book by not sitting in tedious meetings and filling in forms for those I call (in other books): *corporate apparatchiks*.

Semi-finally, I would also like to thank Germany's *Hans-Böckler-Stiftung* that supported – during the 1980s and 1990s – my transition from being a toolmaker in Germany's car industry to becoming an academic.

Finally, I would like to thank the editors of the following non-profit news websites: Countercurrents and Counterpunch for publishing – during 2016 and 2023 – the original contributions that make up the main part of this book. All the articles in this book were published online on their websites (see sources list at the end of the book).

Contents

Introduction

By the time this introduction was written, the media was engulfed with issues that an *artificial intelligence* (AI) could write articles, essay, and perhaps even chapters in a book on Brexit. Before the *real* introduction of this book starts, here is a little taste of what an AI-generated introduction on the issue of, for example, *Brexit and Capitalism* would look like. After a little excursion into the world of AI-written chapters, the *actual* introduction will start. The real introduction ends with a brief overview of the structure of the book and its eight core chapters. But first, here is a little example of what an un-edited text generated by artificial intelligence on Brexit looks like:

Excursion: An artificial intelligence – chat.openai.com/chat – generated writing on "Brexit and Capitalism":

One of the main ways capitalism contributed to Brexit was through the rising income inequality it created. In recent decades, the UK has experienced a growing divide between the rich and poor, with the wealthiest individuals and corporations capturing a larger share of the country's wealth.

This trend was exacerbated by neoliberal policies implemented by successive governments, such as privatization, deregulation, and cuts to social spending. As a result, many ordinary Britons felt left behind and disconnected from the benefits of economic growth.

In the run-up to the Brexit referendum, this sense of frustration and disempowerment was channeled into support for leaving the EU, which was seen as a way to take back control and restore national sovereignty.

Another way capitalism contributed to Brexit was through deindustrialization. The UK was once a manufacturing powerhouse, but in recent decades many industries, such as steel, coal, and textiles, have declined or disappeared altogether. This was due to a combination of factors, including globalization, automation, and the rise of low-cost competitors in countries such as China.

The result was a loss of jobs, particularly in the North of England and other regions that were heavily dependent on industry. This created a sense of resentment and disillusionment among many working-class voters, who felt that the political and economic elites had abandoned them. The Brexit campaign tapped into this sentiment by promising to bring back jobs and revive struggling industries, although it remains to be seen whether this will actually happen.

Finally, capitalism contributed to Brexit through the neglect of certain regions and sectors of the economy. In recent years, the UK has become increasingly reliant on the financial sector, particularly in London, which generates a large share of the country's GDP.

However, this has come at the expense of other sectors, such as manufacturing, agriculture, and regional economies outside of London. This imbalance was exacerbated by austerity policies, which cut funding for public services in many regions and contributed to a sense of resentment and neglect.

The Brexit vote can be seen as a rejection of this economic model, as many voters in neglected regions and sectors saw leaving the EU as a way to shake up the status quo and demand greater investment and support.

In conclusion, capitalism played a significant role in the Brexit vote and the damage done to the British economy. Rising income inequality, deindustrialization, and neglect of certain regions and sectors of the economy contributed to a sense of frustration and disempowerment among many voters, which was channeled into support for leaving the EU.

However, it remains to be seen whether Brexit will actually deliver the economic benefits promised by its supporters, or whether it will exacerbate the underlying problems of the UK's capitalist system.

The Actual Introduction

Well, after three years of Brexit, Al's suggestion made in February 2023 that *remains to be seen was whether Brexit will actually deliver the economic benefits promised by its supporters, or whether it will exacerbate the underlying problems of the UK's capitalist system*, has largely been answered. Just over three years after the UK had left the EU, it is crystal clear that Brexit did not *deliver the economic benefits promised by its supporters.* Instead, Brexit is very likely to *exacerbate the underlying problems of the UK's capitalist system.* As the negatives and false promises of Brexit issued by Britain's conservative party for years and the many warnings had been ignored, it has become more and more obvious, almost every day, that many might also ask the rather legitimate question of, *how could this misery-causing Brexit have been made possible in the first place?*

Perhaps the event that was Brexit – Great Britain leaving the European Union – might be linked to the well-known theorem of *geography is destiny*. Except through what in Europe is called the *Euro-Tunnel* and the British called the *Channel Tunnel,* that opened in 1994, there is no permanent man-made link between the UK and Europe. The UK remains an island. The 50km or 31 miles between Calais and Dover continue to separate Europe from the UK – and this is not only in geographical terms. While there have been people living in what we today call as Great Britain or the UK since about 12,000 years, these people came from Europe. Yet, Europe is also a continent with which the UK has had several wars against with throughout the last three centuries.

One of the more significant years in the history of the UK–Europe relationship was the year 1066. It marks the last time the UK had been invaded by a foreign force. Neither Napoleon's army, nor German troops occupied the UK during World War I and World War II. Upon the experience of a second attack by Germany, European powers sought a way to prevent this from ever happening again. Shortly after World War II and the defeat of German Nazism, European countries agreed on two systems to prevent any future wars in Europe – mostly to deter the Germans from making war. The first of the two solutions became NATO with the task, as it is colloquially known, *to keep the Russians out, the Americans in, and the Germans down*. The second system is that of a European integration and the subsequent European Union.

European integration and what we today know, as the European Union (EU) began with the *Paris Treaty* of 1951 that envisioned closer European cooperation by involving the two war- making industries of coal and steel. This culminated in the setting up of the *Coal and Steel Community* between France, Germany, Italy, Belgium, Netherlands, and Luxembourg. On that, the online website Wikipedia, for example, simply says, *the United Kingdom refused to participate.*

At a very early time of post-war history, the refusal of the UK had set up a pathway of an – at times – rather shaky, if not conflict-ridden relationship between the EU and the UK. This continued when the UK also *refused to participate* in Europe's next step, the creation of the *European Community* in 1957. Yet sixteen years later – on the 1st of January 1973 – the UK eventually joined the European Community. Not long after that – barely six years after becoming an EC member – the staunchly inward-looking, anti-EU-immigration, and zealously neoliberal, Margret Thatcher was elected prime minister of the UK (1979).

This not only marked the beginning of the implementation of Hayek's ideological catechism of neoliberalism – as outlined in his short book, *The Road to Serfdom* (1944) – into political reality in the UK, and elsewhere. It also signified the beginning of a very long period – 1979 to 1990 – of extremely strenuous British relations with the European Union. This included highlights like Thatcher's infamous *"no, no, no"* and her notorious handbag – with a brick inside – thrown into the face of European leaders. British anti-EU politics of a narrow-minded corner shop mentality ended only after her ideological predecessor John Major (1990 to 1997) left *Number Ten Downing Street* – the prime minister's residence. From a European perspective, things only got better – many might say "normal" – after a political change in the UK. It came with the premierships of Tony Blair (1997 to 2007) and Gordon Brown (2007 to 2010) – both Labor Party. Yet, it wasn't going to last.

Gordon Brown and the Labor Party was replaced by conservative Tory prime minister David Cameron (2010-2016). The conservatives had set their minds on Brexit, perhaps even before Minister David Cameron made an election promise to hold a referendum on Britain's membership in the EU. The fateful date of his announcement was on 23rd of January 2013. One year before that, pro-EU advocate Peter Wilding used the term "Brexit" for the first time in @britinfluence – fb.me/256WKGMfF on 15th of May 2012, in which he complained that Britain is, *stumbling towards the Brexit*.

A year later and perhaps in a gross misjudgment of the British mood and a most severe underestimation of the power of Murdoch's nationalistic-conservative press empire which got him elected in the first place, Cameron vowed – perhaps in the mistaken belief that the Brexit referendum would fail – that, if his Conservative

Party wins the next general election in 2015, there would be a referendum on the UK leaving the EU. Cameron won the 2015 election.

Undeterred, the conservative's Brexit politics, Cameron's election-winning promise, and the rather nationalistic Brexit debate had created a deeply divided nation. These divisions only deepened with the actual referendum in 2016. It was further cranked up by Boris Johnson, i.e. BoJo's *"Get Brexit Done!"* election in 2019, and the subsequent exit of the UK from the EU at 11pm or 23:00 (GMT) on the 31st of January 2020. It came with dire consequences.

As the UK left the European Union, substantial sections of British capitalism suffered. Yet, an even bigger problem was the underlying weakness of British capitalism under neoliberalism and de-industrialization. In addition to this, British capitalism had lost – after 48 years – direct access to its most important marketplace: the EU. After decades of de-industrialization and neoliberal capitalism, the remaining British manufacturers were barred from the tariff-free trading regime of the EU's internal market – while European companies and corporations have unhindered access across European borders.

Worse, the promises of Britain's conservatives to renegotiate new bilateral treaties with governments across the world have largely evaporated into thin air. These re-negotiations of trade deal became necessary as previous deals were included in the EU trade agreement. Brexit ended this. Since then, UK deals have virtually made no progress. Furthermore, people will no longer be able to work freely in both economies. British workers can no longer work in the EU and EU workers can no longer simply move to the UK. Simultaneously, all goods exported out of the UK and imported into the UK are now required to fill out significant additional paperwork. Trading goods and services across borders has become significantly harder. After Brexit, companies must check documentations extensively to verify that they comply with local regulatory standards.

For a country that has advocated *free trade* for decades, it no longer, and has made it part of its ideology to justify capitalism, frictionless trade is basically over in regard to Europe. By early 2023, one of the key remaining sticking points was a treaty between Northern Ireland and mainland Britain with the possibility of a new customs' border across the Irish Sea. Worse, the British conservative government also fought tooth and nail to protect the fishing industry. It failed. Ideologically hyped up for election purposes, the reality is that fishing contributes a microscopic 0.04% to the GDP of the UK. Meanwhile, the services sector contributes over 70%.

Of course, most of the UK's financial services are not exported. Yet, the UK's services exports contribute 30% to UK's GDP. Worse, about 40% of its services trade is with the EU – directly. To make matters even worse for the UK, the UK runs a massive goods trade deficit with the EU. This is – in part – compensated by having been able to run a surplus in services trade with the EU. This will no longer work. Currently, the main trade surplus comes mainly from financial and professional services located in the city of London.

In fact, exports of UK financial services were worth about $72 billion (£60 billion) annually compared to imports of $18 billion (£15 billion). Worse for the UK, 43% of its financial services exports go to the EU. Even more daunting is the fact that the Brexit deal with the EU – so far – has done nothing for this vital sector of the UK's economy. With Brexit, providers of professional services have lost their ability to work in the EU. This automatism too, is gone. To make matters much worse, the UK's Brexit deal has failed to obtain Pan-EU mutual recognition of professional qualifications.

This means that professions such as, from doctors and vets to engineers and architects must have their qualifications recognized in each individual EU member state where they want to work. Ending red tape and regulation was promised by Britain's conservatives. What came instead are more red tapes and more regulations. Perhaps the conservative's deregulation ideology and neoliberalism were no more than electoral pitches. In reality, the very opposite has been engineered by British conservatives for those who want to work in the EU.

Simultaneously, the UK-EU deal does not cover access to financial services to EU markets. This will now have to be determined by a separate process under which the EU will either unilaterally grant what is called *equivalence* to the UK and its regulated companies or, secondly, leave UK firms to seek permissions from individual member states. In other words, more bureaucracy – not less.

Over the coming years, there may well be – with a bit of luck but it does not appear to look very promising – what one might call *bit by bit* agreements on trade in these areas. But the UK service sector has ended up worse off for its exports than was the case when the UK operated within the EU. This is set to continue over the forthcoming years. All of this is very serious for Britain's version of capitalism because the UK is basically a *rentier economy.*

A *rentier* economy or *rentier* capitalism describes an economic practice of gaining large profits without contributing to society. A *rentier* is someone who earns income from capital without working. This is generally done through ownership of assets that generate yield – cash generated by assets. For example, a landlord who rents apartments without building them. The landlord does not manufacture anything thus creating no value. Instead, a *rentier* generates income from rental properties, owning corporate shares in dividend-paying companies, and bonds that pay interest.

Rentier capitalism describes the fact that British capitalism depends to an overwhelming degree on its financial and business services sector – and no longer on its manufacturing sector. It is a consequence of de-industrialization that was cranked up by neoliberalism put in place in the 1980s by Thatcher. By 2022, post-Brexit Britain's financial services contributed about 7% to UK's GDP – roughly 40% higher than in Germany, France, and Japan.

Even before Brexit and particularly since the advent of neoliberalism, the UK has become a country of rentiers, investors, bankers, lawyers, accountants, mini-celebrities, and media people, rather than engineers, builders, and manufacturers. As a consequence, the UK has a huge and top-heavy banking sector. Simultaneously, it now also has a relatively small manufacturing sector compared to other G7 economies — Canada, France, Germany, Italy, Japan, and the United States, as well as the European Union.

Beyond all this, Brexit had a substantial impact on working people. With leaving the EU, what the little British labor had gained from the EU's labor regulations is in danger of being eliminated. This comes on top of the fact that Britain is a country that already has one of the most deregulated labor markets and industrial relations in the OECD. For example, one protective EU regulation includes a 48-hour week maximum — which of course is riddled with exemptions so that companies and corporations can "legally" bypass it. The safeguard on the 48-hour maximum ended with Brexit. Brexit will also have a negative impact on health and safety regulations.

Beyond all that and potentially with even more devastating outcomes is the elimination of the EU's regional and social subsidies — the EU's *Cohesion Fund*. Under this, regions with a per capita GDP below 75% of the EU average — for example, Cornwall and South Yorkshire — received EU funding. No longer. This was — and for EU member states still is — designed to move disadvantaged regions towards the average wealth of comparable EU regions. Furthermore, Brexit will end all science funding through the EU. It will also eliminate environmental checks, and of course, above all, it will abolish the free movement of labor. All of that is eliminated or substantially minimized.

By 2020, about 3.7% of the total EU workforce – roughly three million people – were working in a member state other than their own. Since 1987, over 3.3 million students and 470,000 teaching staff have taken part in the EU's Erasmus scientific and educational program. After Brexit, this program excludes Britons from participation. Before Brexit, inner-EU immigration into the UK from other EU countries had been significant. Yet, this also worked the other way around. Many British people are still working and living in continental Europe.

With the UK out of the EU, these British workers are now subject to strict work visas. Contrary to the false promises of UK conservatives, the costs of exiting the EU are greater than the total money – per person – saved from contributions to the EU. These were taxes that British people had to pay to be a member of the EU. On balance, EU immigrants – this means all immigrants, not just EU migrants – have contributed substantially to the UK economy. This contribution comes in taxes – mostly through income tax and VAT – and by filling in low paid jobs in hospitals, hotels, restaurants, farming, transport, etc. This is far more than what the migrants have taken up, e.g. the cost of schools, public services, etc. Unlike the blame –

and, at times racism – metered out by the UK's conservative press, the reality is that migrants contribute positively to an economy. Just like in the USA, Canada, Australia, New Zealand, Germany in the 1950s and 1960s, Argentina in the 1920s, etc.

Elsewhere and also in the UK, that is largely because most migrants are young and often single and help pay pension contributions *for* those British people who have retired. Not too long before the actual Brexit – on Saturday, 1st of February 2020 at 10:00 AM, to be precise – the Brexit referendum of 2016 had already resulted in a relatively severe drop in net immigration into the UK from EU member states. This was spiced up with a rise in anti-foreigner resentment and outright racism, as well as an increase in racially motivated attacks in the UK. At the same time, migration had declined to 50,000 from 100,000 people and it continued to decline during the immediate months and years after Brexit. Overall, three issues contributed to making the UK an unattractive location:

1. the often rather anti-migrant debate, referendum on Brexit, and the actual Brexit;
2. the nationalistic if not chauvinistic and xenophobic ideology of the conservatives; and

3. the anti-foreigner propaganda of Britain's conservative press (Murdoch, etc.).

In economic terms, the decline of skilled migration had only added to the overall loss of national income and tax revenues in the wake of Brexit. Long before Brexit, many of the most sober evaluations of the economic impact of leaving the EU had suggested that the UK's economy was set to grow more slowly in real terms than it would have done if the UK had remained an EU member. In other words, preventing trade from occurring, and reducing or stopping net migration of people would come at a serious economic cost to the post-Brexit UK.

Many mainstream economic institutes – and this also included the Bank of England – projected that there was to be a cumulative loss in real GDP for the UK over the first ten to fifteen years after Brexit. This was estimated to be between 4% and 10% of GDP. This translates into about 0.4% points of annual GDP growth. In other words, even without the Covid-19 of 2020-2023 and even without Russia's war against the Ukraine that had started in 2022, Brexit would have a negative impact on the UK's economy. All this was in sharp contrast to the rosy hallucinations of the conservatives – even though British conservatives knew about what the Bank of England and others said about the negative economic impact of Brexit.

Worse, the economic hit that the UK would have to take after Brexit had a cumulative impact of a whopping 3% of GDP loss per person. In other words, British voters — including those who had voted for Brexit — were set to become poorer. In real terms, this was set to be equivalent to about $1,200 or £1,000 per person per year.

By 2022, the UK's *Office for Budget Responsibility* had calculated that one-third of this relative loss had already taken place. In part, this occurred because of the drop in the pace of business investment since the Brexit referendum in 2016. Since then, domestic businesses had stopped from investing much. To some extent, this was because of the uncertainty about Brexit. In addition, the UK also experienced a sharp drop in foreign investments as the debate about Brexit was cranked up.

And then, of course, there was also BoJo's botched-up response to the Covid-19 pandemic that had decimated business activity. In 2020, the UK had suffered a very large fall in GDP. This was quite unique among major economies — apart from Spain. Worse, the UK recovered more slowly than other countries during 2021. Even unhealthier, British capitalism had already began slipping rather significantly *before* the Covid-19 pandemic started to bite.

In those years, the UK's trade deficit with the rest of the world had widened to around 6% of GDP. Worse, real GDP growth had slid back from over 2% a year to below 1.5% while industrial production was flattening to about 1%. Overall, the UK's rentier economy had weak investments and productivity growth compared with the 1990s and compared to other OECD countries. In the UK, all this was to end with Brexit, so the rosy promises of the conservative went. The UK's conservative government's fairytales claimed that because industry and the financial *City of London* would – after Brexit – finally be able to expand across the world because it would be *free from the shackles* of EU regulation. This promise turned out to be completely wrong, at best. Alternatively, it was an outright – albeit election winning – lie at worse.

Perhaps the plan of the conservatives was to turn Britain – like some little Caribbean Islands – into a tax-free and regulation-free base for foreign multinationals. The UK's conservative government was planning to set up so-called *free ports.* These are geographical areas with little to no taxation. This was supposed to encourage economic activities. Being located geographically within the UK, they exist fictitiously "outside" the UK's borders for tax purposes. Very unfortunately, for the UK's conservative government, studies have shown that *free ports* simply defer the point when taxes are paid. Worse, such tax incentives may also promote the relocation of economic activity – that takes place anyway – from one part of the UK to another. Still worse, tax breaks meant a loss of revenue for the UK Treasury. Finally, such *free ports* can become facilities for money laundering and tax evasion.

In sum, a further deregulated post-Brexit Britain will not restore economic growth, let alone creating good and well-paid jobs for an educated and skilled workforce. In the coming post-Brexit years, such a further deregulated economy would have only boosted the short-term profits of multi-nationals using cheap and unskilled labor.

As shown during the first three years after Brexit, the much-trumpeted Brexit deal turned out to be another obstacle for a sustained economic growth for Britain. BoJo's messed up response to the Covid-19 pandemic, Russia's war against the Ukraine, and, of course, the underlying weakness of British capitalism based on forty years of neoliberalism are all damaging to the UK's economic future. Among the four, Brexit proved to be one of the most significant *extra burdens* for British capitalism, as well as for British households.

Three years after Brexit, the time for *Bregret* had arrived. After the divorce from the EU in 2020, by early 2023, it became clear to the majority of the British people that Brexit was not working. They started to regret Brexit. It turned Brexit into **Bre-**xit + re-**gret** = *Bregret*. Yet, the longer it takes for the UK's conservatives to recognize the great waste of Brexit and potential remedies, the longer instability and economic downturn might last. Beyond all that, the British always had an almost unsurpassed talent for coining neologisms.

After Brexit – the **Br**itish **exit** or break-up with the EU – which took place three years ago – many in the UK – even those who voted in favor of Brexit – started to talk about *Bregret. Put simply.* they regretted Brexit. Far from being no more than just a whim or fad among some nostalgic commentators, *"told-you-so"* analysts, and critics, *Bregret* has become a bitter reality. By 2023, a very clear majority of British people – actually, 57% according to the recent polls – would now vote to re-enter the EU. Interestingly, this is 5% more than originally had voted for Brexit. Brexit became when not even 52% – actually, just 51.89% – voted for Brexit (voter turnout was 72.21%).

In other words, Brexit was made possible by just 1.89% of British voters who pushed the votes to cross the 50% border in favor of "YES" to Brexit. Given the UK's 46,500,001 registered voters, these 1.89% translates into 879,000 votes. Simultaneously, all this also means that 65.6 million people had to leave the EU because no more than 879,000 voted for Brexit – roughly the size of Leeds – plus a handful of surrounding villages. If these 879,000 voters had not voted for Brexit, Brexit would have never happened.

By early 2023, it became obvious that on both sides of the argument, the observation is identical, *Brexit is not working*. Despite the daunting realities of Brexit, former prime minister Boris Johnson (BoJo) has continued to blame Covid-19 and the Russian war for the country's poor economic performance. This is designed to shift attention away from him as he was *the* main instigators of his very own election winning *Get Brexit Done!* By early 2023, his political-rhetorical game of *smoke and mirrors* was becoming increasingly impossible to believe in. Incidentally, by late January 2023, a rather significant Brexit *coincidence* had occurred.

Exactly at the time when the UK's conservative prime minister Rishi Sunak's government was trying to celebrate the anniversary of Brexit by congratulating itself for *forging a path as an independent nation with confidence*, the International Monetary Fund (IMF) published its forecast. According to the IMF, the UK will be the only one country out of the world's major economies to go into recession in 2023. And here it came thick and fast,

> *The UK's economy is the only one that has not returned to its pre-Covid-19 size.*

Unlike the glowing promises of UK conservatives between 2016 and 2020 – the years between the Brexit referendum and the date when the UK actually left the EU – by 2023, the diagnosis was clear. By leaving the EU and by, subsequently, re-establishing customs controls to the EU, Brexit had hampered relations with the EU – the UK's main trading partner. Brexit had amputated a whopping 15% of British trade.

Worse, supply chains had been disrupted and investment had slowed. Labor shortages had intensified with the end of free movement with the EU. By early 2023, inflation was escalated through the rising cost of borrowing following the conservative's disastrous budget decisions during the ultra-short-lived – just 49-days – premiership of Liz Truss in late 2022.

In the end, the politics of the conservatives, including the highly successful pro-Brexit election campaigns, delivered stunning electoral successes, particularly for BoJo in 2019 winning 365 seats compared to Labor's meager 202. All that came at a bitter cost for the British people. By 2023, the well-known phrase of the UK being *the sick man of Europe* that used to illustrate the UK prior to 1973 – the years *before* the UK had joined the European Community – was coming back into public debate.

In addition to Brexit, by early 2023, the UK was also experiencing a series of strikes and social discontent. This had built up after years of neoliberalism, relentless austerity, Brexit, and deliberate underinvestment in public services. All this came based on the *free market will fix* belief of Britain's neoliberal conservatives. By 2023, the UK showed a series of strikes larger than any since the 1970s. On the 6th and 7th of February 2023, another massive strike took place among the 360,000 nurses of the systematically underfunded and privatized *National Health Service*. Health workers demanded a 10% increase in pay. As the workers who make the UK's NHS possible went on strike, the UK's entire health model was being questioned.

Beyond all that, there is the reality of a rather fundamental uncertainty of the post-Brexit divorce from the EU. This was engineered by a rather fanatical determination of Britain's conservatives for deregulation – a euphemism for pro-business regulation. The conservative's ideological and political zeal was to transform the country into a tax-free platform at the doors of the continent and the EU. This too, has failed.

Today, the fabricators of Brexit, the so-called Brexiters – while acknowledging the current poor economic performance – blame all this, not on their very own Brexit, but on the nervousness of their government's willingness to liberalize the economy and break with European rules. Even after three years of continuing failure, some conservatives persistently, staunchly, and undeterredly claim that Brexit provides a *huge opportunity.* This is despite the fact that Brexit has already been discredited in public opinion. By March 2023, conservative prime minister Rishi Sunak still showed little sign of being able to break the Brexit deadlock that his very own conservatives had created.

As for the leader of the opposition – Labor's Keir Starmer – who, by 2023, was the clear favorite in public polls, Starmer began, at least but way too cautious, to acknowledge the damage caused by Brexit. Yet by early 2023, many had started to argue that the longer it takes British conservative politicians to recognize the great waste that Brexit is, the longer it will take to find remedies, and the longer the instability is likely to continue in Europe's oldest democracy. In a sign of changing times, the British have even come up with a new name for those who want to return to the EU, *Rejoiners.* Yet, from a European perspective, the signs do not look promising that the UK can move from *Brexit* – via *Bregret* to – *Rejoining.*

A Brief Timeline of Brexit

2010: PM Gordon Brown (Labour) was voted out of office.

2012: The term Brexit is invented by pro-EU advocate Peter Wilding.

2013: Minister David Cameron made an election promise to hold a referendum on Brexit.

2015: Cameron wins the 2015 election.

2016: The year of the Brexit referendum.

2017: In an election, the Conservatives managed to remain the largest party in the House of Commons.

2018: The Brexit withdrawal agreement is published.

2019: Boris Johnson "Get Brexit Done" election wins conservatives an 80-seat majority.

2020: on 31st of January, the United Kingdom withdraws from the European Union.

2021: As of 1st of January 2021, the UK is no longer in the EU Single Market and Customs Union.

2022: Russia attacks the Ukraine, and the Covid-19 pandemic finally starts to wind down.

2023: In public polling, over 50% of British people say "it was wrong to leave the EU."

The Structure of the Book

The subsequent eight chapters, plus an introduction and a conclusion, outline how and, perhaps more importantly why, the UK has outmaneuvered itself into today's rather unfortunate position of having to live in a post-Brexit world – setting itself apart from the EU, and perhaps even apart from continental Europe. While British conservatives have been the key instigators of Brexit, the first chapter – *Brexiting Through the Media* – outlines that Brexit would hardly have been possible without a pro-Brexit, nationalistic, xenophobic, and semi-racist press.

Just one example might illustrate this. Long before Brexit, the man who eventually pushed Brexit through – BoJo – was a "journalist" in Brussels furnishing, and sometimes simply inventing (e.g. the Italian condom fable), anti-European press stories to be published back home in the UK. Over many years, this had a negative influence on the public perception of the EU by many in the UK.

Yet, Brexit never came unconnected from what is shown in *Brexit, History & Ballot Choice* – the chapter. More to the point of winning some sections of the British public over to the *leave the EU camp*, i.e., the *Brexiters,* is shown how this was done by the analysis presented in the third chapter on *How Brexit Won.* After the conservatives had won the Brexit referendum (2016) and the *Get Brexit Done!* election in 2019, the fourth chapter – *Post-Brexit Truck Driving – a Driver's Report –* provides an early insight into what it would be like to work in a post-Brexit world. This is illuminated by the daily life of a truck driver commuting between the EU and the UK.

The fifth chapter on *The Dark Money and Dirty Politics of Brexit* illustrates one of the key reasons behind the success of the pro-Brexit camp in the UK. It shows how *Dark Money* came to play a significant factor in the 2016 referendum and to some extent, even in the 2019 *Get Brexit Done!* election. As the economic consequences of the electoral success of the conservatives and this includes the Brexit referendum, eventually Brexit started to hit home. This resulted in, as the sixth chapter delineates, early *Brexit Anxieties.* These first hints of growing anxieties about Brexit eventually mutated into *Bregret.*

Not long after these early anxieties about Brexit, the seventh chapter profiles what many people in Britain started to realize, namely that *Brexit Bites Back.* In other words, the negative consequences of Brexit started to bite even into those who had voted for Brexit. Finally, chapter eight – *The Schadenfreude of Brexit* – does not deliver *Schadenfreude.* It is not about this German word outlining the experience of pleasure, joy, and self-satisfaction that comes from learning of or witnessing the troubles, failures, and humiliation of another.

While some might argue that there can – and perhaps even should be – a *Schadenfreude of Brexit,* the economic and political misery of Brexit caused by the conservatives might not be called *Schadenfreude.* The paycheck issued by the conservatives for their electoral victories between 2010 and 2019 and for fabricating Brexit will have to be paid by others.

The book ends with a conclusion that delivers a rather sober assessment of Brexit after the first three years of Britain being no longer part of the EU. It focuses on the years 2016 to 2023. Not just in hindsight, the many dire predictions and warnings issued by many between 2016 and 2023 – including the naked Cambridge economist Victoria Bateman in 2019 (as shown on vimeo.com) – have painted a rather troubling picture of the reality for many, if not for most British people. All in all, the book shows how it was possible that Britain has made Britain poorer.

Chapter One:

Brexiting Through the Media

(Written on 11th of August 2016)

Just a few weeks ago, the majority of the British people voted for **Brexit** – exiting the European Union. Absorbing the shock, the Guardian's editor Katharine Viner delivered an impressive analysis of the media and Brexit, focused on "technology's disruptions (Guardian Weekly 22.07.2016). But there might be a little bit more to the story.

The story of media capitalism is inextricably linked to democracy and what the German philosopher Habermas calls the "public sphere". Historically it all starts with the French philosopher Rousseau's *volonté générale* (the public will) and the French Revolution in which, for the first time in human history, it wasn't us who got starved, killed, brutalized, beheaded, and tortured.

Instead, it was the French-ruling elite that experienced Robespierre's guillotine, quite literally chopping off the head of feudalism. Deeply traumatized by this experience, the European elite still calls it "the reign of terror". Yet what they themselves had done for centuries and continued to do for decades throughout Europe (mass poverty, starvation, killing striking workers, preventing women from voting, etc.) was never labeled in the same way.

The European elite also learned three things from the aftermath of the French Revolution. For one, Rousseau's *volonté générale* constituted a clear and present danger for the "power elite" (Mills) or bourgeois (Marx). Soon, the European elite spent the better part of the 19th century eliminating democracy.

But towards the end of the century, it realized that it could not prevent the expression of the public will in the form of democracy forever. It learned how to use democracy to maintain power when it realized that it could shape the public will rather successfully through mass media, propaganda, and mass deception.

Perhaps one of the first to recognize this was the pair of German philosophers, Adorno and Horkheimer in their "Culture Industry: Enlightenment as Mass Deception" (1944). But it was also American linguist Chomsky and his "Media Control – The Spectacular Achievements of Propaganda" (1991) who highlighted the power of propaganda.

Perhaps the prime example of "mass deception" and the "spectacular achievements of propaganda" remains signified in the person of Rupert Murdoch. Virtually every recent British prime minister got on her (Thatcher) and his (John Major, Tony Blair, Gordon Brown, and David Cameron) knees asking for his media support. Through the control of the media, democracy was no longer a threat but a vehicle for the elite.

In historic terms, once Rousseau's *volonté générale* was controlled by the media, democracy was rolled out in Europe as it helped to gain and maintain power. The elite has always seen democracy as not much more than just "one" way to power – but purely a means, or a tool. Meanwhile, progressives tend to see democracy as a virtue "in-itself" (Kant).

As a consequence, the ideological start-up prime minister of neo-liberalism (Maggie Thatcher) used the media rather skillfully to gain and maintain power when she installed her deeply ideological neo-liberal programs.

As the social cost of neo-liberalism became increasingly strenuous to British society, scapegoats needed to be found. The British elite and its compliant media capitalism found two: migrants (racism) and an anti-Europe stance (British nationalism). Both enabled the elite to shift the blame of the increasingly destructive costs of neo-liberalism onto others. To blame was the migrant (the Paki corner shop) or the distant European monster bureaucracy. This also enabled the elite to continue installing neo-liberalism and winning elections – even though in a slightly modified version under Thatcher's greatest success: Tony Blair.

Being aware of the power of blaming and relying on the assistance of media capitalism, the prime instigator of Brexit – David Cameron – combined racism and nationalism for years to shift the blame onto others while getting elected and re-elected. Britain's Daily Mail, Sun and tabloid-TV were always there building up both – migrants and Europe – as the prime threat to Englishness.

After years of blame-shifting, the media only had to intensify its propaganda during the Brexit campaign and the "spectacular success of propaganda" (Chomsky) was virtually assured. Even though one of the world's smartest intellectuals – Stephen Hawking – recently noted, "I believe it would be wrong to leave the EU" and instead of rational analysis and the better argument, propaganda carried the day.

In the end, Brexit has very clear winners. While David Cameron personally lost his job (a collateral damage), Theresa May – with Boris Johnson (the clown) as foreign secretary – continues to be in power which, after all, is the only game in town. But having shaped public opinion on Europe and migration for decades, David Cameron was able to claim that the British people have spoken and that "we (the Tories) carry out the democratic *volonté générale* of the British people."

For many, it was the Tories that defended Britain against the foreign take-over through migrants and European rule. Now post-Brexit, British neo-liberalism is even freer from the EU's regulatory regime. It can further de-regulate the few remnants of the once British welfare state. And it can better prevent European regulation on tax havens impacting on British capitalism – a small but not insignificant win for David Cameron's personal monetary affairs.

But perhaps there is also a second Brexit winner: the US-citizen and media mogul Rupert Murdoch. Viewed from his adopted home – the USA – taking out Britain via Brexit weakens Europe and thereby strengthens the USA. It also strengthens the rule of the conservatives in Britain and thereby, furthers Rupert Murdoch's ideological agenda. This may be the "banality of evil" (Arendt) but it surely helps Murdoch.

In conclusion, Brexit resulted from an interplay of several factors – Cameron's blame game conducted for years prior to Brexit, Murdoch's media power, the hyping up of Englishness, and decades of the cultivation of nationalism, and racism. All of these managed to out-maneuver the enlightened sections of the British money elite that favor internationalization and globalization. In the end, conservatism and nationalism won. But the British people will have to live with the consequences, as always.

Chapter Two:

Brexit, History & Ballot Choice

(Written on 1st of February 2020)

In a mistaken version of Trump's catchcry, "Make America Great Again", some British voters might have been led to believe that Brexit will Make Britain Great Again. They were convinced that the – never really – good old days of the British Empire would return by voting for Brexit. This is not to be.

Capitalism and history have moved on. You can't go home again. The world has seen three hegemonies of global capitalism emerging during the last three hundred years and then disappear. During the 17th century, the world saw Dutch trading and colonizing capitalism. Holland's capitalism was taken over by British gunboats and slave-trading capitalism. This is not to say that the Dutch did not trade slaves. They did with a vengeance, but that is another story.

In the 18th and 19th century, capitalism belonged to Britain. During those two centuries, Britain established an empire in which the sun never set, so the jingoist myth went. In continental Europe, meanwhile, during the 19th century imperialism meant three rather different things. For German capitalism, it meant unifying the country by customs unions, railways, and military conquest.

Only in the year 1871, following the defeat of France by Prussia, did the cluster of German-speaking states start to come close to what we call Germany today. Wilhelm of Prussia became the new Kaiser of the German Empire, crowned in (of all places) the Great Hall of Mirrors at Versailles. Capitalism demanded a unified economic space. Germany's unified nation (the Reich), however, only coalesced towards the end of the 19th century. Later, German nationalism led to the most horrific excesses the world has ever seen, symbolized by one word: Auschwitz.

But the 19th century meant something different for France. For the French, it meant following the monarchy and the emergence of a revolutionary empire. In Hegel's dialectical terms, manifested in Napoleon's Grand Army conquering "world spirit on horseback" reaching all the way from Paris to Moscow. If only for a brief time, until the emperor's defeat at Waterloo, Europe was politically united, and could thereafter be conceived as a virtual common market, even when the new states became independent

In sum, three significant things happened in the 19th century, as far as Capitalism was concerned. Germany was busy with itself, France was busy with Europe, and Britain was busy with colonizing the rest of the world. In the end, of course, each of those empires imitated its rivals, and smaller states jockeyed for position within the new international order.

This came about contrary to the common belief that British people are reserved, the French talkative and abstract, and the Germans cold, insecure, and obedient. But British imperialism was never reserved. The French were as grubby and grasping as anyone. The Germans pushed into Eastern Europe, built railways, and fought among themselves. It is said that Britain conquered every country it laid eyes on; the French taught everyone to speak French, love French food, and think French feelings; the Germans became idealists, swilled beer, and lusted after power.

After more than a century of British colonialism and imperialism, the British and French empires were in terminal decline by the end of the 19th century. Germany, despite having small colonies in Africa and the South Seas, expanded into a European-centered Reich—swallowing up half of Denmark, impinging on the Austro-Hungarians and establishing economic dominance in the Balkans.

Some say, the sinking of one of the world's most advanced ships, the Titanic in the year 1912, marked the decay of European civilization. Others say, it was World War I (1914-18) that, despite Britain and allies winning, marked Britain's decline, France's weakening, and Germany's inner turmoil in the wake of the Second Reich's collapse. America grew stronger.

By the conclusion of the Great War, it was no longer possible to say that British's manufacturing ruled the roost, but instead thanks to the systematic business principles of Frederick Taylor and Henry Ford's conveyor-belt, assembly factories introduced the so-called *American Century American consumerism.*

Sadly, for British imperialists, then as now, many romantic illusions held about Britain are what they always were, that is, hallucinations. Meanwhile, back in the real world, with India's independence after World War II, Britain's empire was well and truly gone, and the glory days as crown jeweler of British colonialism a mere memory of a phantasm.

In terms of Realpolitik, the industrial and military power of Uncle Sam (the USA) dominated a new era in world history. The 20th century saw the great struggle between three ideologies: Fascism, Communism, and Capitalism in the guise of Democracy, Fascism, Stalinism, and Capitalism. By the end of the last century, it was clear who the winner was: Capitalism, but not necessarily democracy.

At the beginning of the year 2020, it might be safe to predict that the United States of America will carry on being a (and not the) dominant player. Still, it is even more safe to assume that Great Britain (and only precariously as the United Kingdom) without the European Union, thanks to Brexit, will not return to the glorious days of the hegemonic empire. England on its own will never again be a dominant player. John Bull (symbol of the nation of merchants and manufacturers) will not shape the remaining 21st century.

For most people in the UK, the British Empire meant no more than the fourteen-hour working day and child labor in William Blake's Dark Satanic Mills. In other words, the rural workers and the urban proletariat did not go horseback riding with Jane Austen's county gentry and lovely Mr. Darcy. Brexit is unlikely to bring those happy days back, not even for Boris Johnson's upper classmates at Eaton.

Instead of fox hunts and village fetes, British men, and women, then as now, had to fight for a living. They struggled for living wages and campaigned for workplace rights. In 1998, a British case went to the European Court of Justice (ECJ) concerning an English woman who had been dismissed from her job while pregnant. The EJC decided in favor of the plaintiff. Shortly thereafter, Britain's Sex Discrimination Act was re-interpreted and eventually amended.

With Brexit essentially a done deal (more or less, hard, or soft), the EU is gone as a backstop for British Law Lords, and Boris Johnson, furnished with a sufficient electoral win, can proceed to reform (that is, deform) England's unwritten constitution. Some traditional work-place rights, we predict, will be turned back. After Brexit, British women, once again, can be fired for being pregnant, and shoppers can pick up delicious, chlorinated chicken on the way home freshly imported from the USA, as EU food safety rules will no longer apply.

Having lost the security and strength of the EU through *Get Brexit Done*, Britain will find herself rather alone, if not isolated, in dealing with the coming of the five great challenges of the 21st century, challenges defined by people, technology, money, the media, and ideas, to wit:

1. **People:** There will be a continuous flow of people within the British Isles (from north to south, west to east, etc.), to the UK, and out of the UK. Brexit as a done deal (or non-deal) will only marginally alter this process already speeded up during the dreadfully long and sluggish debates. Despite Brexit, or perhaps even because of, the flow of legal migrants, asylum seekers, desperate exiles, and pushy tourists will not stop. Migration has been a feature of Europe for a very long time. Brexit will not stop this. In fact, it might enhance the flow of people.

2. **Technology:** There will be a flow of technology. Since the days of the steam engine, capitalism has been driven by technology. The movement of technology will be in terms of hardware, manufacturing components, technical know-how, and IT. But this movement is unlikely to be

outward. Instead, it will be inward. Britain will become a major importer of technology, not exporter. Even before the bills were passed in the House of Commons allowing Brexit to proceed, manufacturing had already begun to relocate into continental Europe, leaving the UK and this trend will continue and increase. Tesla's new factory is shifting close to Brussels and Berlin – not to Birmingham. This also means that post-Brexit Britain is unlikely to remain a technical, engineering, and information technology center. Continental Europe is a more likely candidate. And why not? It has the size, the infrastructure, and the money.

3. **Money:** There will be a flow of money (national stock exchanges and commodity speculations). London will still be Europe's finance center. But several banks and financial institutions have already started to look for alternative sites inside the EU. Some look at popular destinations with the front-runners being Dublin because of the English language, and Frankfurt because of its centrality, the European Central Bank, and its established banking system. Still, Frankfurt is considered to be boring. Finally, as said in the movie Casablanca, "we will always have Paris" with the greatest

European culture but also a few language problems might be expected.

4. **Media:** There will be flow of information (newspapers, magazines, satellite television channels, websites, the Internet). The English language provides a clear advantage for the city of London, rather than the rest of the UK. Nevertheless, IT's global techno-leader is the USA with GAFMA – Google, Apple, Facebook, Microsoft, and Amazon.

5. **Ideas:** There is also a flow of ideas (human rights, environmentalism, free trade movements, fear of terrorism). Traditionally, Britain has been seen as a strong center for such intellectual enterprises as human rights. However, on a global environmentalism scale, the UK remains a follower, lagging behind the EU, and particularly Denmark. Brexit is set to make this situation worse. Most European countries have understood that Britain's much beloved free market cannot fix global warming. A government capable and willing to operate at an effective level remains to be found. Facing global warming means a big, powerful, and financially strong state, and the UK has just withdrawn from such an entity. Worse, Brexiteers, the British

conservative party, its ideology of neoliberalism, and Boris Johnson all point in the exact opposite direction. Like Trump, they are climate change deniers, or at least trivializers.

All this raises the really big question: with the British empire gone and virtually no chance of returning to it and the five challenges outlined above unsolved, why did the pro-Brexit groups and the Tory Party win on the 12th of December 2019 at all? Perhaps Boris Johnson's slogan Get Brexit Done! provided a convincing frame for enough people to understand the world of politics.

In addition, Boris Johnson is a master of the blame-game. For years, his job was to lash out at everything and anything on the EU. In the case of Brexit, he blamed the holdup on Labor even though opposition arose strongly from within his own party. The results of the recent election show that blaming (or scapegoating) others still works.

In analyzing the defeat, US-democrats, Australia's Labor Party, and Britain's progressives are making the same mistakes over and over again – perhaps a traditional sign of insanity. They still believe in the Enlightenment myth that the truth will set us free. If we only tell the people the truth, they will vote for us. The mass of voters are rational human beings. This is wrong for two reasons: firstly, people do not get the truth.

They get what the Murdoch media (Fox, the Sun, etc.) tells them is the truth; secondly, at least since Kahneman and Tversky (1970s and early 1980s), we know that voters make non-rational decisions. In the case of Brexit and Boris Johnson, they voted against their class interest and for nationalism, if not for outright racism. As for Trump – his base – also voted against its own best interest.

Despite so much evidence to the contrary, many self-appointed election analysts hang on to the *l'idée fixe* that it is irrational to vote against your self-interest. True or not, people do that, and they do it rather often. Otherwise, conservatives would not win elections in most countries as they are at the beginning of 2020.

Consequently, progressives and their election analysts are once again shocked and surprised when voters do not cast their ballots as the pundits predict. These experts start infamous soul-searching, change their leaders, and beat their collective breasts, all without ever understanding what really happened. They fail to realize that whenever conservatives use Orwellian language, for example, they not only tell outright lies to the people and engage in elaborate and covert propaganda. They show their vulnerability. Despite the overwhelming media presence of conservative voices casting aspersions in almost every direction but the right one, this is the strategic flank to attack that is allowed to pass unnoticed.

Another issue progressives fail to realize is the fact that conservatives enforce message discipline. In other words, despite Abraham Lincoln's warning that "You can fool some of the people all of the time, all of the people some of the time, but not all of the people all of the time," they stay on message: "Get Brexit Done!" Everyone knows the chant off by heart now. "Make America Great Again!" – Everyone knows that too. And what do we hear from the other side? From Britain's Labor Party and the US Democrats side: Zilch. A blank space.

Unlike Democrats (US) and Labor (UK), the Tories and the Republicans relentlessly hammer away the same simple message over and over again, until they win. Winning elections isn't a mind game for intellectuals. You win by finding the lowest common denominator: a message everyone understands, everyone knows, and everyone can vote for. It is not a sophisticated eight-course French menu. Instead, it is a bit like driving through McDonalds and being asked "Do you want fries with that?"

Find the food everyone (except us intellectuals) likes and sell it. Don't explain the good, medical, or moral reasons why they should become vegans. The Big Mac is a winning ticket. Conservatives have figured this one out long ago. And so, they win elections: in the USA, in Brazil, in the UK, in Australia, in the Philippines, in Israel, in Hungary, in Poland, in the Czech Republic, in India. The list goes on.

With the backing of the Murdoch press, Trump, Boris Johnson, and their Australian counterpart Scott Morrison (ScoMo) were able to dish up politics in a way everybody could understand and everyone understood. Trump, Johnson, and ScoMo presented cultural stereotypes and framed their single message accordingly. They were also convincing in presenting themselves as father figures who can protect the American / British / Australian people from invading foreigners, including lesbians, queers, transvestites, and post-modernist non-binomials.

This does not mean that progressives everywhere should be like ScoMo, Trump, and Boris Johnson. The opposite is the case. Progressives do not win elections by betraying their identity – by shifting to the right of the political spectrum. This is not what the electorate expects. Instead, progressives need to invent a believable message and stick to it. It needs to be an easily consumable message that has relevant values. For example, taxes are not bad. Taxes means that the fire brigade comes when you need it, that your roads are safe, that the rubbish is collected, the air is clean, and schools and hospitals are working.

In doing this, progressives face two opposing groups. Progressives face corporate and conservative media. Elections are a 2 against 1 (2:1) game. Progressives need to challenge conservative ideologies, such as that a hierarchical society is eternal and that a leader should always be obeyed. These are deeply anti-democratic concepts. Liberals and moderates need to challenge the old-fashioned right-wing idea that to be moral is to be obedient to authority. What makes progressive ideas moral is thoughtful and controlled disobedience.

Challenging the immorality of authority makes one a good person. Progressives also need to destroy right-wing hallucinations, like the rich are good. The wealthy and the influential are not a natural elite. They will never fit through the eye of a needle. The poor are not poor because they lack discipline or are lazy. The poor do not deserve to be impoverished and disenfranchised and they should not serve the whims of the rich.

Today, right-wing thinking is applied to schools and universities. Conservatives know that without a culture war, they cannot win elections. Next to winning significant battles in the culture war, conservatives also have established a significant number of think tanks that hammer right-wing messages on TV, day in and day out. In some cases, they write press releases that go straight into understaffed and underfunded newspapers, radio, and TV stations. They also had *Cambridge Analytica*, they still have Russian troll farms, and most importantly, they also have a polarizing propaganda-machine called Facebook, as well as Twitter (Trump's preferred propaganda tool), WhatsApp, YouTube, etc.

Intellectuals from Albert Einstein to Stephen Hawking have never been on the side of closed-mind conservatives This is the point where progressives make one of their most crucial mistakes. They think the general population is like them. Most people are not intellectuals. They are not trained to develop and understand complex and sophisticated arguments. They are not trained to spot contradictions. The mistake they make is a bit like what happens in group thinking. They assume that everyone thinks like an intellectual. The vast majority does not think like that.

Perhaps none other than Karl Marx understood this. He wrote a book for intellectuals *Das Kapital* (Capital) and he wrote (with his comrade-in-arms' Friedrich Engels) a little pamphlet for everyone else

– *Manifest der Kommunistischen Partei* – Communist Manifesto. Progressives are not going to win elections by producing *Das Kapital*-like programs. The tax program of the Australian Labor party is a great example. It was well thought-out and made a lot of sense, but it was too complicated for the ordinary voter to figure out. Meanwhile, ScoMo's falsehood "Labor is a high-tax party" registered with the punters. He won and Labor lost bitterly. Now we are stuck with him, as Australia burns.

Unlike nineteenth-century Karl Marx, many present-day left-leaning Liberals, Democrats, and moderates appear to be trapped inside their own vicious circle, those who read the same newspapers and hear the same long-winded speeches and analyze the same books, and hence are (at least to themselves) "smart". Hence, too, we get the aforementioned just-tell-the-truth misconceptions.

This fallacy is derived from a non-recognized delusion of the partly educated who tends to think that everyone is an intellectual. As a consequence, many progressives end up talking about political party programs, not values like the right does. They insist on the correct program and policy instead of talking about hard-headed principles and moral values. They hammer these programs even when clear directions are called for.

It used to be said that intelligent people invented the alphabet and intellectuals have been abusing it ever since. Progressives (not only self-identified but vilified as such by their opponents) can become rather regressive—they keep going back to what they once were taught was correct and praiseworthy. They neither listen to what ordinary people are complaining about, hear what their opposition says, and mock what they don't understand.

Ordinary people who work, feel, and think (when they do) in the hard-nosed, nitty-gritty of their own lives, hear not what their educated leaders and would-be governors think they are saying, but what is done and proposed on their behalf, and they can smell out the rat, the stench of irrelevance and pious nothings. Thus, we end up with a topsy-turvy political world where everyone seems to be talking past everyone else. When this happens, the sly and malicious take up their positions and set that world afire with mean-spirited, mendacious, and exploitative policies.

Conservatives (both upper case and lower case), know that they want to change an open and democratic culture into an authoritarian regime. They try to frame all intellectuals as a despicable elite. On the other hand, they have been successful in attracting the poor (rural and urban, out-of-work and under-employed) and poorly educated males.

In America, without such a base, you can hardly win elections. In the UK, Boris Johnson attracted the same kind of disaffected and frustrated voters in the North of England, to the (again!) great surprise of Labor. Trump was quite explicit, shouting to his audience when shouting, "I love the poorly educated." "I love the poorly educated".

Johnson exploited the new reality, that most of the old working class and rural Labor members felt (perceived the image, felt the vibes, although they didn't listen closely and understand the heart of the message) the party had betrayed their interests for those of the urban, highly educated elite. Given the right (right-sounding, right-wing) message, the "base" will vote against their own best interests. And they not only will promise to do so when interviewed or polled, they actually do it at the ballot. And they do so regularly.

Yet when they do it, progressives are puzzled about the question, how could they win? How could they vote for Brexit? Unless progressives get their message right and frame it in a way that everyone can understand, they will continue to wonder why the right wins election after election.

Chapter Three:

How Brexit Won

(Written on 12th of February 2021)

With Brexit in the box, many have started to reflect on what has happened. Looking back is always a bit like what George Bush – or perhaps Karl Rove (he is certainly smart enough) – once said, "We're an empire now, and when we act, we create our own reality. And while you're studying that reality — judiciously, as you will — we'll act again, creating other new realities, which you can study too, and that's how things will sort out. We're history's actors ... and you, all of you, will be left to just study what we do".

In a similar vein, German anarchists used to say, *die regieren und wir protestieren* – they govern while we protest against their government. In any case, with Brexit, British conservatives have created their reality. We are left to analyze it (Rove) and to protest against it. Looking back, there is a clear reason why Brexit won. Brexiters had three ingredients that assure that right-wing populism wins. It wins from Brexit to BoJo (Boris de Pfeffel Johnson), from Modi to Duterte, from Orban to Bolsonaro – the list goes on. What makes them and Brexit win are three things:

1. Politicians: right-wing politicians and their henchmen produce lies, falsehoods, disinformation, myths, conspiracy fantasies, etc.
2. Platforms: online platform providers transmit right-wing propaganda to millions fast and very cost-effectively while eliminating editors, journalists, facts, and truth.
3. Money: well-financed – often through dark money – lobbying institutions, euphemistically labeled think tanks, institutes, agencies, astroturf organizations, etc., lobby governments and the public for right-wing causes.

Brexit had plenty of all three. It had right-wing politicians like David Cameron promising a Brexit referendum, Theresa May pushing Brexit, and BoJo's Getting Brexit done! Pro-Brexiters also created a strong, highly targeted, and very strategic campaign using social media rather aggressively.

Finally, pro-Brexit lobbyists ran a sophisticated campaign featuring the accidental misinformation but mostly focusing on deliberate disinformation, outright lies, fibs and falsehood. In short, the Brexit campaign had almost everything the right-wing propaganda playbook offers.

With Dark Money coming in by the truckloads, the demagogues of Brexit were able to overspend on their campaign significantly exceeding the legal limit. For the Brexiters, it was simply an All-Out War against their perceived enemies – Britain's quality press, the Labor Party, most economists, the EU, the remainder campaign – and most of all, it was a campaign against facts and figures as well as the truth.

Yet, the Brexit campaign never focused on converting the British public. Too many people favored remaining inside the EU. Targeting the entire UK would have been a hopeless operation. Consequently, Brexiters focused on those they thought can be persuaded to leave the EU – those that could be easily manipulated and persuaded. They are called 'persuadables' – a marketing term that has entered political campaigning.

In the case of Brexit, BoJo's right-wing and right-hand man – David Cummings – identified Brexit's persuadables early on. BoJo's mastermind saw these as a group of about nine million people being between 25 and 55 years of age and living mostly outside of London and Scotland. In other words, BoJo's clique knew that people in the city of London would not support Brexit, and neither would the people of Scotland where 62% voted to remain inside the EU. This meant that the Brexit campaign could not focus on them. They were seen as unpersuadable.

Instead, the Brexit campaign would focus on two things: the persuadable and onboarding – another marketing term. Onboarding seeks to convert sympathizers into committed supporters, financial contributors, and – preferably – into active Brexit campaigners. The onboarding strategy of the Brexit campaign consisted of three steps:

1. People were enticed to click online advertising placed on Facebook, for example. The idea was that such clicks would automatically direct them to a pro-Brexit website, the Vote Leave website, for example.

2. Once on a pro-Brexit website, visitors were tempted to leave their personal details which were to be used for further campaign planning and micro-targeting.
3. In a final step, people were invited to donate to the Brexit campaign and/or become a volunteer supporting Brexit through real political action.

The tripod of right-wing politicians, the willing executioners of the Internet, and Dark Money handlers allowed the pro-Brexit team to engineer a very strategic campaign. Consequently, each step of their onboarding campaign was planned, tested, and checked. Nothing was left to chance. Messages that went out and onto Facebook were tested beforehand. Those messages that failed to achieve a set target were reformulated or discarded. Often, pro-Brexit messages were re-worked until they converted enough people to the cause of Brexit. The measure used is called the *conversion rate*.

In one plan, the Brexit campaign even offered $50 to anyone correctly predicting the winner of a soccer tournament. The marketing plan was to entice seemingly unpolitical soccer fans into the manipulative orbit of Brexit rather successfully. To enter the $50 competition, people had to leave their data on the Brexit website. The soccer competition data was fed into Brexit's ever-growing database, creating a welcome supply of personal data that was instrumental in campaign planning and targeted messaging.

Overall, the Brexit campaign collected data of about 120,000 individuals. Brexit's "Vote Leave" campaign also started an App for smartphones reminding their friends to vote in the Brexit referendum. By the Brexit referendum on 23rd of June 2016, roughly seventy thousand messages were sent via this App, contributing to the victory of the Brexit campaign.

Thirdly, there also was David Cummings' infamous Waterloo Strategy. The Waterloo campaign delivered a pro-Brexit advertising blitz during the last days of the referendum. It was designed to collect undecided swing voters. Someone in the Brexit campaign nailed it by saying, "we spent a shitload of money right at the end".

Indeed, the Brexit campaign was spending about $2 million in the last week before the referendum on Facebook advertisements and videos. By US standards, $2 million isn't much money. But for rigidly controlled non-money-based election campaigns held in Europe, this is a rather significant sum of money – mostly dark money.

Like many other political advertising campaigns, the Brexit campaign knew that ads work best the closer they are launched to an election day or in the case of Brexit, to the day of the referendum. It hits voters almost on the way to the voting booth, and it targets the unsuspecting voter who had not spent much time thinking about the issue of the day. Besides such media strategies, the subject and content of the Brexit campaign focused on three overarching messages:

1. **The Political Lie:** the falsehood that the UK was spending £350 million ($480 million) per week on the EU and that this money could be better spent on health and education once the UK left the EU.
2. **The Fear:** fear was created by telling the British people – falsely – that soon Turkey, Macedonia, Montenegro, Serbia, and Albania would join the EU, bringing a wave of migration to the UK. One of BoJo's ministers even claimed that the UK could not stop Turkey from joining the EU. It was plain wrong, but it was good propaganda, and it worked.
3. **The Nationalism:** the final propaganda item came as Take Back Control. It falsely promised to take back control from the EU. Once this was done, the UK could reduce migration.

All three were targeted disinformation. They were all false, but they were good propaganda or public relations as it is called nowadays. This is the PR side of the Brexit referendum. On the lobbying side, the following happened as perfectly outlined in Howard's Lie Machines.

The UK Electoral Commission found that pro-Brexit – Vote Leave and *BeLeave* – had breached the UK's campaign finance law. Vote Leave spent £449,079 ($620,000) in excess of the statutory limit, and *BeLeave* knowingly spent £666,016 ($920,000) more than the legal limit. The commission fined both organizations.

In other words, playing by the book doesn't pay. Pro-Brexiters did not play by the book, exceeded the limit on what they could legally spend and won the Brexit campaign. Years after the Brexit campaign won, they received a slap on the wrist. That was it. Just as Karl Rove said, "we make history, and all you can do is, analyze it". The pro-Brexit campaign made history, and years later, we can analyze what was done.

Just as Rove implied, years later we can even speculate that hypothetically, if the Brexit campaign stuck to the legal limit, it would have stopped campaigning in the dying days of the Brexit referendum. Perhaps this might have changed the outcome of the Brexit referendum. On the other side of the Brexit referendum was the Remain campaign. The Remain campaign stuck to the legal limit on campaign financing – and lost.

At the end of the successful Brexit campaign consisting of right-wing politicians, online platforms, and dark money, the referendum's result was surprisingly narrow. Pro-Brexit received 51.89% and Remain got 48.11%. Despite all the (dark) money spent and all the lies told, the Brexit campaign just scraped in by a relatively slim 1.89% margin.

In other words, Cummings managed to convert roughly 1.2 million – many came from the targeted group of 9 million. If slightly more than 600,000 or about 6.7% would have voted against Brexit, Brexit would have been dead. But Cummings, dark money, and clever online marketing won the day.

This gave the UK the pro-Brexit referendum that the British conservatives had been craving. In the subsequent "Get Brexit Done!" election of 2019, BoJo only managed to get yet another narrow election victory. If 51,000 voters shifted their votes across forty seats, Boris Johnson's victory probably would have been destroyed.

In short, Brexit is the outcome of two narrow victories for the Brexit campaign in which right-wing politicians were seeking de-regulation through the backdoor by eliminating the EU. The Brexit team successfully used compliant online platforms that transmitted the three great lies of Brexit: a) £350 million per week goes to the EU; b) the conjured-up fear of migration; and c) nationalism's take back control – control that after Brexit has moved from the EU to BoJo – but not to the British people.

All this came with a strategic, well-choreographed, and generously financed Brexit campaign of mis- and more importantly, disinformation that reached and manipulated millions of voters. In the end, the Brexit campaign was effective in four ways:

1. The pro-Brexit campaign highly targeted – not the British people as a whole – but a selected group of persuadables. It also targeted voters in the final days of the Brexit referendum.
2. Using the newest advertising tools, better data, and online platforms allowed the Brexit campaign to engineer enough impact that shifted a few voters needed into their favor.
3. Carefully fine-tuned messaging based on sophisticated testing delivered a high success rate for the Brexit campaign.
4. The carefully formulated and texted messages of the Brexit campaign hit a group that it needed to hit: the persuadables. That is how Brexit was done.
5. In short, right-wing politicians, willing online platforms, and plenty of dark money had set a ruthless right-wing propaganda

machine of mass deception in motion that
delivered Brexit.

Chapter Four:

Post-Brexit Truck Driving
– a Driver's Report –

(Written on 12th of February 2021)

It is Saturday morning in Dagenham, East London and for truck driver Johan Most, Brexit means waiting. It was the Saturday after Britain had left the EU. Lorry driver Most is feeling the dire consequences. He has been on the road for six days. Actually, he wanted to stop in Dagenham only briefly to pick up his customs papers. Barbara

Windsor is the UK customs agent who was supposed to get his official papers ready.

Ms Windsor receives him on the second floor of the freight forwarding building behind a plastic screen – a Coronavirus protection. Ms Windsor had to disappoint the truck driver. The documents for the kitchen appliances which Most is supposed to bring from North Wales to the German city of Hannover are still being processed. Ms Windsor could not say when they would return from "up there," as she puts it.

Johan wears his work clothes, grey jeans, dark blue sweater, and neon yellow vest. He looks resignedly over the parking lot. Tomorrow, Most's wife celebrates her 39th birthday. He actually wanted to be back home tonight. If Ms Windsor doesn't knock on the driver's truck door with the papers in the next few hours, it won't work. Most continues waiting.

On 1st of January 2021, a new border in Europe was created with the UK's exit from the EU. Truck driver Johan Most is one of those who can directly feel the consequences of this decision.

Every day, Johan watches the flow of goods passing through Europe. He is part of a cross-Europe delivery stream – one of those who moves it along. When he talks about his career, it always includes the history of European integration. It has changed the lives of many people bringing many benefits.

In 1990, when Most became a truck driver, those were still the golden days of long-distance transport. Without GPS, without electronic control of the permitted driving times, without tracking from the central office, without a mobile phone— only with a paper folded map and a hand-written delivery address, off drivers went on their own. Being a trucker meant freedom back then.

As usual, Johan Most would now be on his way to and from Great Britain with his truck. There is a ritual from this earlier time that is important. If Most is overtaken by other trucks, he would signal the overtaking driver with a light horn. The rear of the vehicles which are often more than seventeen meters long, can hardly be seen through the side mirrors. In the dense traffic of the London ring, the ritual is a real help. As a thank you, the overtaking truck flashes. It would create small "light show" against the loneliness of the road.

Well, what do you know, Barbara Windsor, the customs agent, didn't knock on Most's window on Saturday. Nor on Sunday either. The driver must remain in England. He stands with his blue jumbo truck, 18.75 meters long. Where is he? He is at a truck stop in East London. The service area is so crowded that some trucks are parked in bus- and car-lanes. Today, Most will spend his fourth night there.

Supplies are slowly running out. Under his bed in the driver's cabin, he had a freezer compartment from which he could take out food to be heated up in a microwave while being on the road. It usually contains ham, margarine, cheese, gouda, cucumbers, tomatoes, ready-made soup, and multi-grain bread.

But today, there is hot food. If Most pays £37 for parking instead of £35, he gets a £10 food voucher for a nearby fast-food restaurant. Most goes to Burger King. He orders chicken and bacon using the voucher. The waitress tells him that he can also have the "double chicken menu" without additional payment. Nice, says Most, not everyone does that anymore.

The year 2005 ended Most's golden years. The logistics industry was in transition. In 2004, Poland, Estonia, Latvia, Lithuania, Slovakia, Slovenia, the Czech Republic, Hungary, Cyprus, and Malta joined the EU. Many companies started to outsource their logistics to Eastern European freight forwarders.

Most's employer also wanted to save costs. Most and his four colleagues were twice dismissed and twice their dismissals were overturned by Germany's labor court. European regulations had protected him and his colleagues. But the company didn't let up. Most was proud to cling to his job. But eventually, like many others, Most quit his job.

The timing was bad. Nobody hired drivers on good terms anymore. Most was faced with a stark choice: either take a poorly paid job continuing as an employed truck driver who can no longer pay the home loan for his house or become self-employed and try to earn enough money on his own to keep his house. Most decided for self-employment. He got a refrigerated truck with his savings. As a subcontractor of a large forwarding company, he moved fresh meat from Portugal to Ireland, ice-cream from Denmark to Spain.

Meanwhile back in the UK, Most is still queueing in line for a Coronavirus test at the truck stop. It is the second time in four days. These tests are only valid for up to 72 hours. Most's first test has already expired. The British government has set up a white container and two blue pavilions for the testing. Two large posters hang on the container, "UK's New Start. Let's Get Going". The British government is promoting Brexit among waiting truck drivers.

Most of the time, Johan Most stands in line in silence. Fifty-eight other drivers wait with him. Behind him, a slim Polish, and a Croatian in a blue jacket with white collar. They talked in broken

English. One asks Johan how long he has been waiting for his customs papers? Four days, utters Most. In the morning the forwarding company called him. The papers are here, he is finally allowed to go.

The three men exchange ideas. The Polish man says he earns as a base wage €950.- For this, the company pays a premium and expenses, usually bringing him to €2,400 a month. In case of illness and pension, however, it looks bad for him. His employer pays social security contributions only on his base salary. Most earns a little more than his Slovenian colleague with expenses for every day he drives and performance bonuses for months without sick leave.

John Most is sorry for those who have been on the road for weeks, sometimes even months at a time, and who earn less than he. If all drivers went on strike for one day, we could achieve something, Most says. Equal pay for equal work, no matter what nationality. He would like that.

Supermarkets would remain empty; parts of the economy would come to a standstill. But as things stands, he can't even talk to most drivers about what they had for breakfast yesterday. At 4pm, after four hours of waiting in an ice-cold wind, Most gets his second Corona test result: negative. He doesn't like to imagine what would have happened with a positive test result. Quarantine in the truck's cabin for sure.

On the way to the Eurotunnel, Most passes a checkpoint. A woman in a rain parka and warning vest asks for his Corona test. Currently, only truck drivers with a negative Corona test are allowed on the last highway towards the Eurotunnel.

When Most drives, he often phones his family, and sometimes, Hans. Hans was once a young colleague of Most's. For three years, Hans drove to England with Johan then he found a girlfriend, and the constant absence became too much for him. Hans quit. Now Hans has a job where he is at home at about 5pm on most evenings. Johan thinks of himself somewhat as Hans' mentor. When Hans told him that he was broke, Most advised him, If possible, get some other work. Most cautioned the young man; you don't have to do much wrong these days to get kicked out.

In 2008, shortly after Johan Most had purchased additional trucks, his clients no longer paid on time. Often, they came up with only half, a third or even only a quarter of the agreed amount. It was the time of the Global Financial Crisis. Most's bank did not want to lend him more money to compensate for the failed payments. Most therefore went bankrupt in April 2008.

He lost his job, his house, and many friends. Most says, I certainly didn't do everything right on the business side of things. But to this day, he is convinced that the forwarding company also shut him down because the competition from Eastern Europe was cheaper.

When Most talks about the year 2008, it still upsets him today. That's when I exploded, he says. When he applied for social assistance without a job and with four children, he was told that he had no claim for help as a self-employed person. After an appointment at a counseling center, he was helped with €200 per week for him and his family. He was unemployed for two and a half months. Mentally, he was down. Some days he barely got out of bed. Eventually, though, he found a new job.

Johan Most started driving for a subcontractor. On Monday afternoon he left his apartment and on Saturday afternoon he returned home. During the day he had to sleep in rest areas. It was summer and it was hot. His truck does not have a stationary air conditioning system. He hardly got any rest. After a few weeks, a letter arrived from the German welfare office. Since he was unemployed for less than three months, he must pay back the €200 support per week he had received. Most paid the money back to Germany's welfare office in small installments.

The alarm clock on his cell phone rings. Most was still asleep at 5am and he had slept badly. Now, he desperately needs a cup of coffee. He puts a pot of water on the gas stove and takes out a brochure from a drawer in the dashboard. It is intended to prepare drivers for post-Brexit customs controls. Most reads the directions. But he still doesn't really know what's coming after Brexit. He starts the engine and heads for the Eurotunnel which is nine kilometers away.

In May 2012, Most started a new job at Schinderhannes Ltd., a shipping company. Since then, he travelled to England and throughout Europe many times. The job is exhausting but people at Schinderhannes Ltd. are decent in this rather tough business with low margins and long hours. "My wage is always there on time on the 10th of the month, sometimes even earlier," Most says. For him, the position at Schinderhannes Ltd. is a safe haven after the last few turbulent years.

Johan Most approaches the Eurotunnel. The check-in is surprisingly uncomplicated. Passport and Corona test are checked twice, once by British officials and once by French officials. Then the condition of Most's truck is briefly checked. He no longer must present the customs declaration; it is stored in the system and is read out via its registration plate. Most is allowed to roll his truck onto the train that will take him back to the EU.

For Johann Most, the Eurotunnel is a towering achievement. It runs 175 meters below the waves of the English Channel, from the white cliffs of Dover to the French mainland. It is almost 50 kilometers long and takes 35 minutes to pass through. If you drive through the Eurotunnel today, the mobile phone even shows the lowest point.

That's one side. The other side awaits you in Calais. The truck terminal there looks like an open pit mine converted into a high security wing. Streets and tracks are surrounded by four-meter-high white metal fences with wire mesh at the top. The entire area is illuminated by yellow and white spotlights. A four-meter-high concrete wall, one kilometer long, separates the terminal from the place where hundreds of refugees had set up a make-shift camp until 2016. In Calais, it seems that the EU is at war.

Since its opening 25 years ago, Most has driven through the Eurotunnel more than 1,500 times. When he approaches the Eurotunnel from the European side, his attention slowly increases hundreds of kilometers before his arrival. He and his colleagues have instructions not to stop in Belgium and France except for refueling. The danger is too great that desperate refugees could cut their way into the interior of the truck, hide on the axles, or climb into one of the spare parts boxes under the vehicle.

If the traffic runs smoothly to the Eurotunnel site, Most has it made for the time being. He can relax. If there is a traffic jam in front of the tunnel, however, the real competition starts. Refugees dart in and out of the lines of trucks, looking for ways to climb inside unnoticed. In his locked driver's cabin, Most constantly looks into the side mirrors, trying to scare potential passengers off by his looks and hooting of his horn.

For many drivers, these hours mean stress every time. In the terminal, the trucks are searched again with dogs and, if suspected, also with a scanner. Nevertheless, if a refugee makes it to England on Most's truck, he is in danger. In a situation like this, *nobody believes you when you say that you didn't notice anything*, he says.

Just before Most crosses the border into Germany, he has one more thing to do. He goes to the gas station and buys a cup of coffee for himself and his wife. If you ask him about truck driving, he has to laugh and says, I have seen many motorways. For most of them, truck driving remains the same old business, but going into the UK is now more difficult and dangerous. Will he keep doing it, you may ask. Well, what else is there to do?

Chapter Five:

The Dark Money and
Dirty Politics of Brexit

(Written on 5th of February 2021)

When an investigative journalist asked a British voter in the British town of Sunderland, "Which way will you vote?" the man replied, "I want Brexit." When asked why, the man said, "Turkey would soon join." He then talked about how millions of Turkish workers could soon be coming to the UK in search of jobs. In reality, of course, Turkish EU membership is no more than a very distant possibility and that millions of Turkish workers might arrive in the UK legally is pure propaganda. When asked where he had heard about all this? "Facebook," the man replied. And with this, my dear readers, the murky story of Brexit's dark money and dirty politics begins.

In Sunderland, a whopping 60% voted to leave the EU in 2016. Many UK voters that year were made to believe that they would take back political control from a seemingly monstrous EU, thus rescuing their beloved British homeland from the clutches of a gigantic bureaucracy across the Channel – a monster that simply does not exist. Overall, there maybe four elements that gave Brexit the upper hand:

1. ultra-conservative tabloids favoring Brexit;
2. a well-crafted Internet campaign by the pro-Brexit camp;
3. conservative and, above all, nationalistic Tory politicians; and finally
4. plenty of dark money.

Dark money is a rather new term, an insidious neologism, meaning funds that come from unknown sources that are highly influential in politics. Dark money supposedly gives the cadre of the super-rich and their many surrogates the means to shape politics. In the USA, the Koch Brothers' "Toxic Empire" remains the most suspected source of dark money manipulating UK politics. Until the death of David Koch, his mysterious empire had spent more than $1.5 billion on Republican political causes.

Dark money also goes hand in hand with right-wing dirty politics and digital disinformation. It signifies a paradigm shift in political communication. Via Facebook and adjacent echo-chambers, political prejudices, xenophobia, chauvinism, nationalism, racism, anti-Semitism, etc. are confirmed and reinforced daily. Right-wing populists like the current Prime Minister of the United Kingdom, Boris *de Pfeffel* Johnson, are swept into office knowing that repeated lying is no barrier to the highest office. Donald J. Trump, the former president of the USA, and many other right-wing populists who circle around him, would agree.

By the time of Brexit, for the first time in UK history, more money was spent on digital communication than on any other form of political advertising. This resulted in an invisible pro-Brexit media blitz. Britain's right-wing nationalistic and pro-Brexit tabloids could barely keep up with it. Right-wing tabloids do not need dark money, but dark money fueled the pro-Brexit campaign in 2016 and Johnson's "Get Brexit Done" election in 2019.

British tabloids are extremely powerful. In 2019, just three companies – the Daily Mail and General Trust, Reach, and Murdoch's News UK – controlled 83% of the British newspaper market. Only the secretive state of North Korea comes close to such numbers!

Crucially, in his early career, Boris Johnson – or *BoJo*, as his friends call him – featured as a tabloid reporter. He was not much more than a story inventor. As such, he was sent to Brussels as a leading Eurosceptic and came back to the UK to peddle his lies. BoJo, the reporter is best known for the Italian condom invention, a story he simply manufactured out of thin air.

Yet it fit right into his, the conservative party's, and the tabloid's right-wing stance directed against government intervention, whether it comes from the UK government or the EU's faceless bureaucrats. The break-away-from–the EU campaign, however, needed money. Lots and lots of money. Among the many dark and not so dark organizations setup to support Brexit, the "Vote Leave" organization had, at some point, more money than they could legally spend. Yet spend they did. And that's how dark money fueled Brexit.

Another Brexit organization called *"BeLeave"* received (from "somewhere") an astonishing £675,000, almost a million US dollars. The cap on spending in a UK constituency is £15,000 or $20,000. In other words, BeLeave collected – by British standards – an outrageous amount of cash for its pro-Brexit campaign. From unknown or unstated sources.

When "Vote Leave" was fined £61,000 ($83,000) for breaking the law, the fine was barely a tenth of the money "Vote Leave" had been given. In other words, the fine was no fine at all. One of the most prominent backers of Brexit and organizers of dark money is (the aptly named) Aaron Banks. He was fined £1,800 ($2,500). Banks is estimated to own between $100 and $250 million. One can imagine how shaken he was by a $2,500 fine. His dark money, we presume, went to "Vote Leave."

Since about six in ten voters in the UK use social media, it paid handsomely for "Vote Leave" to spend 98% of its money on digital advertising. Internet advertising allowed Brexiteers to target those who are known as *persuad*ables, i.e., middle-aged to older people in a particular and often rural and with no university degree. Brexiteers rightly thought that these potential voters were highly susceptible to political ads such as those claiming that millions of Muslims would soon arrive in the UK, a propagandistic falsehood that was broadcasted during the final hours of the Brexit campaign.

Simultaneously, the conservative minister Penny Mordaunt told the BBC that Britain could not veto Turkey's membership to the EU. This was patently not true. The fake news came despite the fact that Turkey's membership plan has been on ice for many years, if not decades. Something so petty as the truth did not stop Brexiteers like Banks from spreading fear. At the same time, African diamond-mining Banks registered donations of at least £8.4 million ($11.5 million) to various anti-EU causes. Banks is a man with pockets deep enough to run an entire political campaign – and in the case of Brexit, he almost did.

Once a reporter asked Banks about his mis- and disinformation campaign on Brexit. Banks snapped back, "It isn't meant to be informative. It's propaganda." With that, BoJo's Brexiteers ran an astonishingly nasty campaign appealing to voters' vilest instincts. The Brexit team had access to a great amount of voter data. For its misuse of such sources, "Leave.EU" was fined £120,000 ($165,000) in February 2019, three years after it had won the Brexit fight in 2016. It was, as George Bush once said,

> *"we act, we create our own reality. And while you're studying that reality – judiciously, as you*

will – we'll act again, creating other new realities, which you can study too, and that's how things will sort out. We're history's actors...and you, all of you, will be left to just study what we do".

As for Brexit, Brexiteers had acted, they had indeed created a reality. And while academics, intellectuals, journalists, and commentators studied the reality of the 2016 Brexit Referendum which Brexiteers won by a slim margin of just 1.89%, the pro-Brexit team acted again, creating yet another new reality. It created the "Get Brexit Done" myth that came with BoJo's election in 2020. This new reality was one you can study too, as Bush would say. Bush would continue by saying, *that's how things will sort out itself.* Brexiteers became history's actors! "And you, all of you, will be left to study what we do."

Later, Britain's watchdog also fined "Leave.EU" another £70,000 ($96,000) for a range of other offences. On appeal, however, the fine was reduced to a Mickey Mouse sum of £4,000 ($5,500). The watchdog, too, would be called a traitor and enemy of the people, a classical line of ultra-nationalistic demagogues.

Perhaps the key to all this might not even be dark money and fines that came years too late and are way too small to make any impact. The key is propaganda. When truth and disinformation, lies, and deceptions become so hard to disaggregate, many voters will decide to believe nothing at all. That is the precise moment when propaganda triumphs. Once truth is eliminated, politics becomes reduced to a partisan battle in which anything goes. Dirty politics reigns.

The ultra-nationalistic North-Irish and Eurosceptic Democratic Unionist Party (DUP) chipped into Brexit with the ability to spend up to £700,000 ($960,000) on the Leave.EU campaign. Beyond that, a stealthy organization called the "Constitutional Research Council" (CRC) had donated £435,000 ($600,000) to the Brexit cause.

Dark money flowed generously into the coffers of the Brexit campaign. Just two days before the Brexit referendum, the CRC donated a further £334,993 ($460,000) to the DUP which, by that time, was not much more than a front organization, and that allowed the Leave.EU squadron to exceed any legally prescribed spending limits. Not much later, the DUP supported Britain's Conservative government. In return, it would get £1bn of concessions, mainly for infrastructure and health spending in one of Western Europe's poorest regions. Overall, it is pretty safe to say that dark money is a cancer in our political system.

But as the late-night commercials say, "wait, there is more". It got even better for Brexit when the pugnacious tycoon James Goldsmith put £20 million ($27,5 million) of his own fortune into Eurosceptic politics. His press secretary was no other than Priti Patel, who would later become infamous for a string of scandals. Scandal-prone Patel links up rather nicely to a top contender when it comes to scandals inside Britain's right-wing politics: BoJo's propaganda ace, Dominic Cummings.

These guys were on the side of still another powerful, stealthy but hardcore anti EU outfit that is deceptively labeled "European Research Group" (ERG). The ERG quickly became a Brexit sect. Members of the ERG even demanded that British universities list academics who were teaching about Brexit, a move that the East German Secret Police, the Stasi would support. Worse, ERG's henchmen were able to spend £340,000 ($470,000) of taxpayers' money on anti-EU activities between 2010 and 2018. In short, taxpayer funding was crucial to the ERG's pro-Brexit success. What else? Dark money also came in via StandUp4Brexit.

Overall, the success of the ERG demonstrates how a fringe and well-disciplined lobbying outfit can pull British politics into a right-wing direction. Anonymous private funding (dark money) enabled the ERG to push their anti-EU agenda very effectively.

Almost self-evidently, when it comes to dark money and dirty politics, right-wing think tanks are never far away. Many of these so-called *think tanks* are no more than corporate funded lobbying organizations with the double function of influence-peddling and propagandizing or, better yet, public relations (PR) as it is called nowadays.

Of course, there are the usual suspects like the Heritage Foundation, as well as the Koch's Atlantic Bridge pushing a right-wing anti-EU agenda. Dark money comes from the likes of the Kochs (environmental vandalism), Philip Morris (100 million smoking deaths in the 20th century), ExxonMobile (environmental vandalism again), and the now bankrupt National Rifle Association (NRA)–another link to direct killing.

Much of this came with a hefty dose of ultra-nationalism if not imperialism. It was spiced up – or "sexed up", as the former British Prime Minister Tony Blair would say – with romantic hallucinations about Britain's imperial-colonialist past. This was euphemistically re-framed as "Global Britain." In this ideology, post-Brexit Britain is riding towards wealth and power. However, the immediate reality of post-Brexit Britain looked rather different.

Undeterred facts or reality, UK's right-wing clings on to the CANZUK delusion of an alliance between the UK, Canada, Australia, and New Zealand. The *idée fixe* of an Empire 2.0 was based on the UK's Secretary of State for International Trade, Liam Fox's phantasy of signing forty trade deals "the second after Brexit", as he puts it. As with so many pro-Brexit lies and deceptions, this too never actually happened. Instead, the Brexit referendum and the "Get Brexit Done!" campaign were well-financed con-jobs that, in the end, delivered no more than a 1.89% majority for Brexit in the 2016 referendum.

Worse, BoJo still lives in a private league with corporate financiers who stand to profit handsomely from Brexit. The prime minister's own sister, Rachel, agreed. Meanwhile BoJo's father applied for French citizenship days after his son had pushed Brexit through. The rich and powerful get international passports – the poor get Brexit.

Yet, BoJo's Brexit was supported by British businessmen, like vacuum cleaner tycoon and Leave.EU backer Sir James Dyson, who no longer produces his machines in the UK. Nationalistic Brexit was also strongly supported by the US citizen Rupert Murdoch's right-wing tabloids.

For the more nationalistically oriented faction of British capital, Brexit was a golden opportunity to shred EU regulations. Based on the neoliberal ideology of de-regulation which, in reality, means pro-business regulation, they financed Brexit openly and through dark money. In their ideologically shaped world, things like "PlanA+ Creating a Prosperous Post-Brexit UK" meant vacuuming up wealth from the middle-class to the super-rich. Meanwhile, broadcasting the ideology of trickle-down economics smoke-screened what is actually being done.

To tilt the UK even more towards the right-wing, the Grand Old Dame of the BBC herself wasn't immune. Academics who analyzed BBC news and current affairs' output found that in 2009, when Labor was in power, left-and right-wing think tanks appeared on the national broadcaster in almost equal measure. By 2015 – one year before the Brexit vote in 2016 – conservative think tanks were twice as likely to be called upon. This is how propaganda works.

Worse, in 2015, the right-wing Murdoch's tabloid Telegraph featured a pro-Brexit vision called "Change or Go" on its front page four times in a single week. With dark money, right-wing politicians, Internet echo-chambers of the "Digital Gangsters" as Geoghegan calls them in his book *Democracy for Sale*, right-wing think tanks as well as right-wing tabloids, the Brexit referendum's

1.89% success looks rather small. Yet, it was enough to push Britain out of the EU.

David Cameron who was Britain's prime minister who initially called for the referendum and was shocked by the results, once said, "We know how it works," implying that dark money and influence peddling, as well as corporate lobbying, "wield tremendous power over UK politics." Indeed, many inside Britain' right-wing know all too well how it works. Dark money, right-wing front organizations, and shady Internet outfits like Cambridge Analytica play an increasingly controlling role in politics. Their money, support from tabloids, and free access to Facebook, among other things. can multiply the lies told by BoJo.

Recall that BoJo's career started with a lie about King Edward II, a fib that cost him his job at the Times. Perhaps as a positive tick on BoJo's CV, along with his cannon of anti-EU lies – such as the alternate fact of Italian condoms – continued for years. All of this led to the big lies he painted on his pro-Brexit bus. In Boris Johnson's latest incident, he was caught out lying to the Queen when proroguing Parliament in late 2019. Not a good show in class-ridden Britain where the lower classes remain loyal to Her Majesty.

Beyond all that, right-wing politics is aided by the UK's archaic electoral system. In 2019, under the first-past-the-post counting system, Britain's Conservatives won 56.2% of Commons seats with just 43.6% of the vote. A shift of just 51,000 voters across forty seats would probably have wiped out Boris Johnson's "stonking" majority entirely. It would have made BoJo's "Get Brexit Done!", engineered during the winter of 2020/2021, impossible.

In other words, the Brexit referendum came with a 1.89% majority (2016) and the Get Brexit Done! (2020/2021) when the UK actually left the EU squeezed through with no more than 51,000 votes. Two rather microscopic wins for which the entire UK will have to pay a bitter price in coming years.

Overall, Brexit shows how dark money and right-wing dirty politics can – based on two very slim electoral margins – shape Britain for years to come. Long before the faithful Brexit referendum, in a fight between right-wing politicians, eager to win parliamentary elections meant to serve the people, played the nationalistic, xenophobic, and often racist card.

Right-wing tabloids, being corporations themselves, supported the neoliberal ideology of de-regulation via Brexit. In addition, a targeted Facebook campaign of dirty politics followed. In this way, all the forces of greed and fear poured in dark money to finance the entire setup of dirty

politics that gave the nation what it most certainly
did not need or want: **Brexit**.

Chapter Six:

Brexit Anxieties

(Written on 7th of January 2021)

In 2016, the former British Prime Minister David Cameron's *l'idée fixe* of a referendum on Brexit slowly became a reality. The Tory's faithful plan was that Brexit would make Britain a strong independent trading partner with other nations. The British people were told that Brexit would strengthen the UK as a global political player. The promise was, and still is, that the UK, as a single entity, would be in a much better position when trading with the EU, the USA, and China.

Supported by the pro-Brexit media and the Murdoch Press, Boris Johnson's infamous Brexit-painted-bus proclaimed these lies and deceptions, what Chomsky once called the *Spectacular Achievements of Propaganda*, won the day.

In June 2016, 52% of the British people voted for Brexit. By 1 January 2021, the UK finally exited the EU. After forty-seven years of EU membership and seemingly never-ending Brexit negotiations, it happened but Brexit has not ended.

The final period of seemingly never-ending negotiations was eventually over. For the fifth time in a row, a British government carried through its rather illusive promise of the UK becoming a global Britain. So far none of the UK's Tory governments fulfilled its many Brexit promises. Like many people on New Year morning, Brexit caused some very serious hangovers. Today Brexit looks still a bit untidy. Perhaps Brexit might even shrink the UK to a significantly smaller country, as Scotland seeks independence.

According to UK's Ministry of Foreign Affairs, the transformation from EU member state to its *l'idée fixe* of a so far unseen economic bonanza, means that the British government will have to invest rather heavily into global relations. In the hallucinations of the UK's conservatives, a post-Brexit rule-based international order will present Britain with an opportunity to present itself as open and confident on the world stage. Among the many promises is Prime Minister Boris Johnson's delusion that the UK will flourish as a prosperous free trade nation on an almost unimaginable scale.

Apart from grandstanding announcements like these, not much has been achieved. Instead, many of Mr *de Pfeiffel* Johnson's promises for a great future for the UK stand in sharp contrast to the fact that his beloved United Kingdom has just given up a time-honored access to the world's largest free trade area – the European Union (GDP: €16.4 trillion). Anti-Brexiteers claim Brexit was completely unnecessary.

Undeterred, the British PM made a deal with the European Union tied up with a neat pink bow on Christmas Eve. The result: after 1 January 2021, the UK-EU trade became even more complicated for the British and the EU.

Every economist and many non-economists know that the UK's dependence on the EU is much greater than the other way around. In this game, size matters. Put simply, the EU has size. The UK does not. Even during the last few months with

Brexit looming, Britain's conservative government had been unable to produce any advantageous agreement with other industrialized nations. The much-acclaimed free trade deal with – whom? – is still a mere mirage.

Yet Johnson's UK remains in good condition – well, so far. The UK has retained some power to assert itself on the world stage. It is still the fifth largest economy in the world. It is still the core of a fifty-four-nation encompassing the Commonwealth. It has one of the five global nuclear powers even though in economic terms this counts for very little. And finally, the UK has a permanent seat on the UN Security Council. On the eve of Brexit, the UK was still in a privileged position. On the downside, it already had all these advantages while a member of the European Union.

Overall, then, UK's current position is still based on historical advantages that were, if anything, strengthened through its EU membership. Brexit came with a certain magician's puff of smoke and a silly romantization on the part of Brexiteers. These pro-Brexit advocates made something seem to appear romantic that wasn't romantic at all. Unsurprisingly, Brexit is a step into the unknown future – not into the glorious past. Britain will have to work out its future role in Europe and in the world.

In 2021, the British will get several opportunities for this. In the new year, the UK will assume the G7 presidency. It will lead an exclusive club of the largest democratic industrial nations. In this role, Britain can invite Australia, India, and South Korea to take part. It can strengthen these democratic powers opposed to authoritarian economic powers – above all China. It is possible that Britain might be able to move the G7 to a G10.

Furthermore, the UK will be hosting yet another important diplomatic event. The UN Climate Change Conference known as COP26. This will take place in Glasgow in November 2021. As a city in Scotland, Glasgow's people are not happy with Brexit. Polls show that the majority of Scotland's population does not support Brexit.

During the last three months before Brexit came into effect, 39% of UK people said that the Brexit decision was right, while a strong 49% stated that Brexit was wrong. Beyond that, Britain remains divided over Brexit.

In a December 2020 poll, 34% were against re-joining the EU, 32% would back an application to re-join the EU and a whopping 34% said "I don't know". This is very different in Scotland. On the day of the 2016 referendum, a whopping 62% of Scots voted to stay in the EU (38% voted for Brexit).

Brexit therefore might even lead towards Scottish's independence.

Meanwhile, back in the UK and Boris Johnson's promises to the contrary, Britain's influence will be smaller in many areas. Again, size matters. In the future, the UK will have to align itself with larger economic powers to offset the EU. In Europe, the EU will set the tone – not the UK. In his EU negotiations, Boris Johnson already abandoned all ambitions not to adhere to the EU's labor, social and environmental standards.

The Tory plan to hit the English working class hard, does not seem to be materializing. Mrs. Thatcher's ghost is still rolling over in her grave. Things will be similar is other areas. In short, the negotiating power of Great Britain is much diminished.

Complicating further negotiations is the fact that the British conservative government has turned out to be a very unreliable partner. Negotiations with the EU since 2016 have shown as much. Instead of solid negotiations, the opposite happened. There were shifting ideas, reversals, omissions, and untruths by the string of UK prime ministers. To the annoyance of EU negotiators, these flip-flops had become almost a routine. Internationally, this has been sending largely negative signals to any future trading partners.

Inside the UK, some British people might have already asked themselves three key questions:

- After the 2016 decision to leave the EU, did London's stock market go up or down?;
- Did the value of the UK's currency (£) decline or increase?; and finally,
- Have house prices in London gone up or down?

An interesting Example in Boston

Undeterred, people in the northern city of Boston, voted to leave the EU. Located one-hundred miles north of London, Boston voted for Brexit by a margin of 76%. Yet now in 2021 in the first days after the end of Brexit's transitional period there is no real joy – only worries in the pleasant little town.

In fact, on 1st of January 2021, what an overwhelming majority of Bostonians had voted for, four and a half years earlier came into force. Along with the rest of the UK, Boston was withdrawn from the EU's single market and customs union. Today, as many of the Brexit-voters walk through the half-empty winter streets of their city in Lincolnshire, they don't feel as if a good dream has come true.

Instead, many Bostonians feel the very opposite. "We don't think the UK-EU deal is good", many have said, while others in Boston have moaned, "we don't see how we will benefit from this". What's more, many Bostonians now suspect – quite rightly – that Britain will continue to adhere to many EU rules in order to trade. A wholesome few speak rather clearly when it comes to Brexit expressing unhappiness with Britain's Brexit politics. "This is not the Brexit we voted for!"

As if that weren't enough, during the Corona pandemic, many Bostonians have lost jobs in local companies. These newly unemployed face a much diminished social welfare state after years of Thatcherite neoliberalism turbo-charged with austerity. As a consequence, many in England had been paid less and less. Wage stagnation and the consequent insecurities are taking their toll. Many worry whether their children will be working in unsecured jobs, or any jobs at all; whether they will ever be able to afford a decent house or flat; and whether they will live a safe and healthy life.

Some people in Boston have already suffered greatly, more than their fair share. The blame has shifted toward migrants from EU countries settling in the UK. Quite a few native Bostonians have been made to believe that migrants have overloaded the local infrastructure and pushed down salaries.

Xenophobia, nationalism, and even racism turned the blame away from Neoliberalism and towards an external factor: the EU and its migrants. Propaganda obscures what neoliberalism does. It deliberately targets the only institution able to secure reasonable wages: trade unions – acknowledged even by the International Monetary Fund. Because of this, leaving the EU will not solve the problems of the British economy caused by neoliberalism and austerity. In fact, it will exacerbate them.

Yet the still picturesque medieval town of coastal Boston is considered a Brexit stronghold. A whopping 75% of its residents voted to leave Europe in 2016 – more than anywhere else in the UK. Today, local conservatives are desperately trying to explain away Brexit's overwhelmingly negative consequences, and claim, too much has changed in the last twenty years, implying immigration. How much is too much?

In 2001 Boston's residents were 98% white British. The next census ten years later showed that about 10% of the 64,600 Bostonians were born in Eastern Europe, 90% were white and British. Most of the migrants came from Poland, Latvia, and Lithuania. Despite the city being 90% British, the *l'idée fixe* is that *migrants are bad* is a rather recent concept pushed by right-wing populism.

For years, migration has been seen as being good for the economy. The USA, Australia, Canada, etc. have proven this. The OECD, for example, believes that the overall impact of migration remains rather small. It argues that an increase of 50% in net migration of the foreign-born generates less than one tenth of a percentage-point variation in productivity growth. Small but still positive. In other words, it is not migration but neoliberalism and austerity – home grown in the UK – that have contributed to wage stagnation and the rise of the precariat.

Yet, Boston needs every single migrant. In a local family business, which grows flowers just outside of Boston, about forty local employees are from Eastern Europe. The company's boss believes that he needs every single migrant. Without those migrants, there will be no flowers, no business and perhaps not even the food that ends up on the plates of the British people every day. As in many industrialized countries, it is the migrants that do the harvesting.

Brexit is set to exasperate these problems. Post-Brexit, there will have to be a new migration system. It will apply in the UK from 1st of January 2021. Under the new system, if people seek to work in the UK – whether they are EU citizens or not – they will need to earn points. Applicants need to demonstrate good English language skills and having a local job offer with a minimum salary of £20,480 per year in an industry with an acute labor shortage.

Local employers in Boston meanwhile, fear that many companies in the agriculture industry could go bankrupt if these rules are strictly applied. Local employees earned between £25,000 and £30,000 a year. But not with a 40-hour contract. They would have to work up to 55 hours a week. Local people who are willing to do this are very few. As a consequence, local employers hope that most of Eastern European employees will remain.

Indeed, many have already submitted applications for the right of residence. A government pilot project will allow seasonal workers to come to the UK for six months. Yet, local employers see a new danger rising. They fear an increased bureaucracy and negative currency exchanges – weakened by Brexit. This might make England rather unattractive for migrants in the long term.

On the shift from an EU bureaucracy towards increased home-made British – more forms to export goods, etc. – Johnson simply said, it is a tragic reality. He did not mention that this is something he has advocated for years and created himself.

It is all the more astonishing that some local employers and small business owners voted for Brexit in 2016. Rather mistakenly, they were led to believe that Brexit would end EU bureaucracy and the much-feared red tape. Many also thought that Brexit was about Britain escaping the dictate of the EU – a common hallucination induced by the right-wing press and by right-wing populism.

Even today, some in Boston would vote in the same way as they did in 2016 – that is, to leave the EU; although many small business owners in and around Boston are preparing for a stony path ahead. Local businesspeople expect rough road to go for at least 12 to 18 months.

Most local business owners also know that they will not get immediate benefits from Johnson's Brexit agreement. On the eve of the full impact of Brexit, some local products are still no more competitive on the domestic market than those imported into the UK. In general, many in the agricultural business are more concerned about competition from non-EU countries than from the EU.

Meanwhile, many Eastern Europeans working in Boston see Brexit in a rather relaxed way. Some believe that the UK is leaving the EU because they have been there for too long. Several non-UK workers have been living in Boston for years.

However, for a long time, these workers did not believe that the final break would come, and that Brexit would be carefully and gradually implemented. Now they are starting to feel the consequences in a rising flood of xenophobia.

Others have secured the right of residence in the UK which is still a pre-Brexit arrangement. Eastern Europeans say they are friends with their English neighbors. Yet on New Year's Eve, there were no public celebrations in the city of Boston, a small city with strict Coronavirus requirements. Even local Brexit voters and supporters have not celebrated the divorce from the EU. Some even believe that the UK should have left the EU four and a half years ago and astonishingly without an agreement.

However, locals are no longer irritated by Brussels. Now they are irritated by Prime Minister Boris Johnson. Some locals openly say, *"What a joker!"* Boris Johnson always wanted power, wrapping himself in a Churchillian rhetoric. Some locals in Boston believe, we bet people in Europe are laughing at him now. They have been laughing even before Johnson's false Italian condom claim.

Chapter Seven:

Brexit Bites Back

(Written on 12th December 2022)

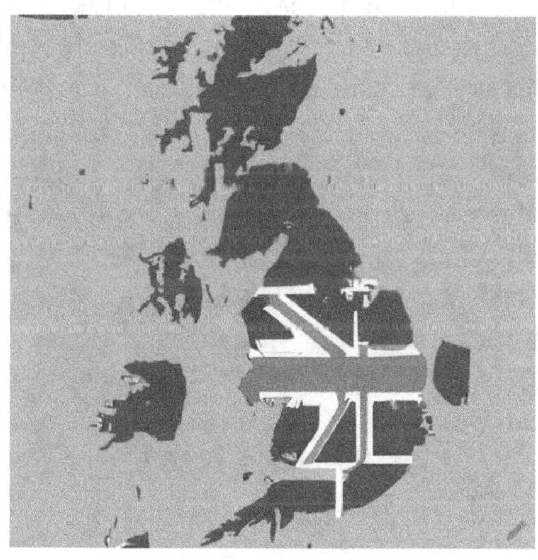

In recent months, British public opinion on the issue of Brexit has shifted. Many people in Britain are becoming more critical of Brexit. With the help of plenty of dark money, Murdoch's press, and the gross misjudgment of a conservative prime minister, the UK held a referendum on Brexit (the British exiting from the European Union) in 2016.

51.9% voted for Brexit. The policy of leaving the EU was confirmed in the UK's 2019 election. And, on January 31, 2020, Britain officially left the EU.

With that, Britain was free from the illusionary shackles of the supposedly un-democratic EU. Self-determination and democracy were put back into the hands of the British people. Strangely, the UK's current prime minister – Rishi Sunak – was not democratically elected by the British people, nor was his predecessor Liz Truss – both conservatives.

Well, at least Brexit stopped the migration of undocumented individuals by boat across the English Channel, right? Not quite. In fact, the opposite happened after Brexit. In 2022, up to November, more than 40,000 people had crossed the Channel in small boats. This was the highest number since these figures began to be collected in 2018. In 2021, the total was 28,526 people, while in 2020, it was 8,404.

Worse, the UK economy is going downhill. This, it seems, also fuels growing anti-Brexit attitudes. Recently, and this came for the first time, British media and even some conservative politicians began saying rather openly that Brexit might have been a mistake.

To get out of their self-engineered troubles, some British politicians are now suggesting the adoption of the so-called Swiss Model, a new paradigm on how to structure the UK's relationship with the EU.

According to the Swiss model, the UK would have to do whatever the EU tells it to do – without any right to participate in EU decision-making governing the EU's €15tr economy. Like Switzerland, the UK is not a member of the EU. It is outside the EU's 450 million people. This occurred because Brexit has shown that, when you put up trade barriers to your most powerful neighbor, you will get hit hard. All this came just as the nude Cambridge economist predicted in 2019. She was spot onl

Almost three years after Brexit, the economic development of the UK – in comparison with that of other G7 countries and the OECD – shows that the consequences of Brexit can no longer be ignored. The country is falling behind the EU and the OECD economically. Yet, Britain's conservative press has created the false idea that the Tories are good for the economy. What is worse for the conservatives is that their traditional excuses – the Covid-19 pandemic and the Ukraine – don't seem to wash any longer with the British public.

The silence on the B-word – Brexit – seems to have been broken. Today, the B-word can be said again. The economy in the United Kingdom is so bad that

Brexit can no longer be denied as a major cause of the current misery.

A few years ago, Boris Johnson was the UK right-wing populists' man. He was the Tory prime minister who ensured there was a hard Brexit. After rafts of scandals, he is no longer in power. His immediate successor – Liz Truss – failed bitterly. After that came the current prime minister, Rishi Sunak, together with chancellor of the exchequer Jeremy Hunt. Both politicians are more pragmatic at the UK's Brexit rudder.

Only a few weeks ago, Britain's leading and very conservative newspaper, The Times, carried an article headlined "Britain mulls Swiss-style ties with Brussels". In it, The Times writes that the British government is considering how it could bring Britain closer to the EU.

In contrast to hard-Brexit UK, Switzerland has direct access to the EU's internal market. Unlike the UK, it also pays the EU, complies with EU regulations, and accepts the free movement of people. In a referendum in September 2020, the Swiss confirmed their model.

Today, some suggest that a frictionless trade with the EU is only considered realistic if the UK, like Switzerland, has access to the EU's single market. However, Britain wants access without the free movement of people, despite a severe labor shortage in the UK.

Even though the EU had already rejected this in 2019, London is still hoping for an EU-UK compromise in the long term. Increasingly, the devastating impact of Brexit can no longer be hushed up by the British government.

Meanwhile, Sunak and Hunt need to get British fiscal policy and the British economy back on track. Their hard Brexit makes this very difficult, since the UK is no longer part of the EU's single market and customs union, and exports have been declining.

Interestingly, UK government ministers now want to remove as many trade barriers with the EU as possible. The plan is to do this over the next decade. Yet, all this should – in the hallucinations of the British Tory party – be done without the UK becoming a member of the single market.

Meanwhile, Sunak has postponed the UK's planned membership in the Trans-Pacific Free Trade Area. He did this in order not to block the UK from a closer trade relationship with the EU. In other words, the EU is already shaping British trade policy, even though the UK is no longer part of the EU. Perhaps BoJo's grand idea of a post-Brexit Global Britain has been quietly retired, like his infamous Brexit bus.

With the dying hallucination for a Global Britain, there is no longer any talk of a trade agreement with the United States, which would also complicate EU-UK relations. However, the UK's re-approaching the EU remains politically hyper-explosive inside Great Britain. Improved EU-UK relations are unimaginable for the Brexit hardliners – particularly after they propagated their phantasm of Brexit-wonderland for half a decade.

When it comes to the inevitable – Britain needs the EU – the Tory government immediately paddled back while sticking to its *Brexit-is-great* script, even though this is so clearly not the case. At a recent conference of the powerful and extremely influential Confederation of British Industry, the UK prime minister made it clear that there would be no case where the UK would comply with EU regulations. Goodbye, Swiss model.

More importantly, Sunak did not respond to the CBI's request to follow the Swiss model. He also rejected the CBI's idea of allowing more immigration from the EU. The CBI sought this to ensure that British companies would no longer suffer so much from their acute labor shortage. All this is bad for the UK as it will increase its economic problems.

On the other hand, some of this might well be good for Sunak and the hard-Brexiters. The PM depends on the support of Brexit hardliners inside his own party. Perhaps, this internal party support is more important to him than the campaign financing by the CBI for Sunak's Tory party.

Meanwhile, the proponent of a hard Brexit – Tory boss Jacob Rees-Mogg – never grows tired of stressing that the public voted for Brexit and that the public wanted to end the free movement of people. There should be no more discussion, he argues.

Lord Frost – the mastermind who failed as the UK's Brexit negotiator – said that any kind of Swiss model with EU regulations was completely unacceptable. Meanwhile, Lord Cruddas – the British billionaire and donor to Britain's conservative party – threatened that he had enough money and influence to thwart the plan to move towards a Swiss-style relationship with the EU.

Worse was to come. Right-wing populist Nigel Farage, who was extremely instrumental in campaigning for hard Brexit, tweeted, "this level of betrayal will never be forgiven. The Tories must be crushed."

At least partly because of Nigel Farage's successful Brexit campaign and the UK's successfully leaving the EU, living standards in the UK have fallen and are set to fall even more in the next two years. Out of fear of being attacked by the UK's right-wing press, the hard-liner Brexiters, and pro-Brexit Labor voters, opposition leader Keir Starmer has been reluctant to call for a Brexit model different than what Britain has today.

Meanwhile, Labor's opposition spokeswoman for financial affairs, Rachel Reeves, admitted the obvious about the Brexit mess, "The Brexit deal the government secured has cost our economy dearly." At the same time, Greens MP Caroline Lucas said,

The huge elephant in the room is #Brexit. Hunt didn't once mention how it contributed to 4% productivity drop, 15% trade drop, 6% food price increase, lower wages, workforce shortages & highest inflation in G7.

Labor is proposing a trade agreement with the EU that would overturn some trade barriers. But fearing the pro-Brexiters, Labor's Sir Keir Starmer has strictly rejected a UK membership in the European single market. Meanwhile, UK prime minister Sunak and his Tory off-sider Hunt have been accused, by the pro-Brexit hard right, of having hijacked the government in the interests of the EU.

And the hard pro-Brexit right has powerful allies, such as the staunchly nationalistic and right-wing Daily Mail headlining, Rishi Sunak and Jeremy Hunt killed the dream of any Brexit dividend stone dead. The reactionary tabloid argued that Hunt and Sunak are about to destroy what Brexit should have brought in terms of benefits: a country with low taxes and high wages, where the economy and the public experience growth. This is a delusional mirage, given the current economic situation of the UK.

Facing severe economic hardship because of Brexit and rising energy costs, Sunak is forced to turn towards a kind of European-style social democracy. The recent economic development of the UK – in comparison with other G7 countries and the OECD – shows that the consequences of the Tories' hard Brexit can no longer be ignored.

The UK is falling behind economically, and this can no longer be excused with the pandemic and the Ukraine war. According to the most recent forecast by the UK government's very own Office for Budget Responsibility (OBR), the standard of living of Britons will fall by a whopping 7.1% over the next two years. The biggest fall on record, this negates the income progress of the past eight years. Brexit bites back!

Worse, data from the OBR and the European Commission show that no European country will fare as badly during next year as the UK. Its gross domestic product is set to fall by 1.4%. The UK is the only one of the G7 countries with an economy that has not yet reached pre-pandemic levels.

The latest survey by YouGov shows that 56% of respondents believe that Brexit was a mistake. Of the people who voted for Brexit in 2016, a whopping 70% still think that this was correct. Overall, one in five who voted for Brexit in 2019 now thinks it was the wrong decision. In other words, a whopping 20% of all Brexit-voters thinks what they had done was wrong.

The British economy has suffered sustained damage as a result of Brexit – something hard-liner Brexiters like Sunak refuse to acknowledge, blaming instead the so-called Covid-19 legacy and the Ukraine.

Meanwhile, Michael Saunders, the former member of the Monetary Policy Committee of the Bank of England, suggests, "If we hadn't had Brexit, we wouldn't be talking about an emergency budget like we had this week."

From an economic point of view, Brexit is like kicking the soccer ball into your own goal. In the wake of all this, public opinion in the UK is becoming more critical of Brexit. Lord Deben (Tory) said, "Our situation is worse in every area because we've left … people now know the terrible damage what leaving the EU has done."

Perhaps many people voted for Brexit in 2016 and again in 2019 out of frustration with the general situation and for all sorts of other reasons. Many might have been misled by a well- engineered propaganda campaign by Murdoch's powerful press, nationalistic right-wing populists like Farage, and hyper-narcissistic and power-hungry politicians like Boris Johnson.

Now they are starting to realize the damage Brexit has caused to Britain. In the UK today, the B-word is being talked about again. Yet, Tory politicians that got Britain into the mess seem to know no way out. Then again, would the EU take the UK back?

Chapter Eight:

The Schadenfreude of Brexit

(Written on 2nd of February 2023)

Decades ago, a German word entered the English language. The word was Schadenfreude. Schadenfreude is the experience of pleasure, joy, and self-satisfaction that comes from learning of, or witnessing the troubles, failures, and humiliation of another. Yet, this German word has no direct translation.

Some might argue that people might feel Schadenfreude about Brexit – when the UK left the European Union. They feel pleasure and joy about the troubles, failures, and humiliation that the people of the UK have brought onto themselves. Brexit came with a slim majority of just 1.89% of voters. It was this 1.89% that got Brexit across the line of 50% when 51.89% of the British people voted for Brexit on 23rd of June 2016.

Just about two years after Brexit – the UK's separation from the EU came into effect. It was exactly on 31st of January 2020, at 11p.m (GMT) when the United Kingdom officially withdrew from the European Union. The separation – known as *Brexit* – was supposed to bring prosperity to the UK. By contrast to the overblown pro-Brexit election announcements of a glorious future, Britain's economy is in fact clearly lagging behind the rest of Europe.

Unlike the propagandistic pledges of his three conservative predecessors – May, BoJo, and Truss – the fourth and current Tory prime minister – Sunak, a multi-millionaire is preparing the British for more problems. The UK has clearly missed its target for trade agreements set for the year after Brexit.

Less than two-thirds of the foreign trade volume have so far been covered by post-Brexit trade agreements. Originally, the conservative government in London had set a target of 80% for new trade contracts by the end of 2022.

Yet, the possibility – as a sovereign state freed from the shackles of the EU – that the UK can conclude its very own trade agreements, was one of the central promises of Brexit.

According to the latest official figures available, only 63% of foreign trade is covered by such contracts so far. The Tory government had set high goals but achieving them seems out of reach.

Instead of trade deals, the UK's conservative government is claiming to be "ready to continue negotiations" with, for example, the United States – a rather humiliating outcome after two years.

In the meantime, the conservative UK government "was busy working towards" (!) reducing trade barriers for British companies. As negotiations with the EU and the USA aren't going anywhere, the Tories announced that they would focus on deals with India, the Gulf states, Canada, Mexico, Israel, and the Indo-Pacific.

On the map of UK trade partners, one has a hard time finding these countries because they are rather insignificant in terms of trade with the UK. The UK's top trading partners are the USA,

Germany, Ireland, the Netherlands, and France – of which four are EU countries.

The excuse of the Tory party is that trade agreements are complicated. In reality, the rest of the world does not see trade with the UK as important as the UK's very own Brexiteers made everybody believe – including themselves.

In other words, not everyone – in fact nearly no-one – is waiting patiently in a queue wanting to sign a trade deal with what the Tories sold as "Global Britain". The fairytale of "Global Britain" was another hallucination that made Brexit possible.

The humiliating failure of British conservatives is especially true in the case of the USA which was always considered to be the "main prize". Despite Bojo, Truss, and Sunak's hallucinations, negotiations with the USA government and its current president Joe Biden are currently not very promising.

On the EU side, things are no better. The dispute between London and the EU over post-Brexit trade rules for Northern Ireland makes the situation more complicated. In many cases, those few trade agreements the UK has reached with other countries have simply been a 'cut-&-paste' job from a time when the UK was part of the EU. Today, conditions are much worse for the UK (e.g.

those with Australia and Japan) than they were when the UK was still part of the EU trade regime.

According to a recent survey, the trade pact with the EU does not bring the British companies the expected benefits. In a survey by the British Chamber of Commerce, more than three quarters of the companies surveyed said that the Brexit deal does not help them to increase their sales. In fact, according to these data, 56% of companies have problems with the new trading rules.

On the second anniversary of Brexit, the Scottish government is also renewing its criticism of the British's exit from the EU. Scots believe that the damage caused by Brexit will only continue to grow. In the two years since the end of Brexit's transition period, Scotland have not seen any advantages in leaving the European Union.

Despite the well-crafted PR myth that "they can run the economy", UK conservatives have made sure that the British economy is basically on the wrong track. Worse, British conservatives staunchly follow Maggie Thatcher's TINA: there is no alternative – to Brexit.

Yet, in the all-important 2016 Brexit vote, the Scots had voted against Brexit – by a large majority. Meanwhile, the current British Prime Minister Rishi Sunak is trying to further soften up the British about the persistent Brexit problems. These are the problems that his party – the conservatives – have created in the first place.

Recently, he was forced to admit that 2023 will present "us" – of course, there is always the rhetorically important "us" – with challenges. These are called "challenges" to avoid words like problems, misery, failure, etc. Yet, economy Uber manager – the conservatives – have created all of these problems. Sunak's public relation statement was followed by a rather meaningless, *the government I am leading puts its priorities first.*

The rhetoric is continued by blaming others. Brexit isn't mentioned by Sunak, naturally. Instead of Brexit, Sunak blamed the Russian war of aggression against the Ukraine for the UK's severe economic crisis with high inflation and recession. The conservative's propaganda seeks to imply: the economic misery we have created has nothing to do with Brexit!

The myth making continues with, the whole world will be hit by this, Great Britain is no exception. What remains unmentioned is that – unlike any other OECD country, Britain suffered from a double whammy: Brexit and Russia's war.

What is also hidden in the conservative's speech is that most experts see the consequences of Brexit and fundamentally wrong economic decisions of the ruling Conservative Party as a decisive factor.

In other words, the acclaimed master of the economy – the conservatives – have made sure that their own goals have not been achieved. Contrary to the "we run the economy hallucination" of the conservatives, the British pound is actually losing its value while exports are lagging.

Worse, the political party that claims to fight red tape and bureaucratic hurdles has actually made sure that trade is further paralyzed by even more paperwork – not less – after Brexit. Worse, Brexit is also a disaster in so many other respects – from growing racism in the UK to a marked decline in student exchanges, and less scientific exchange with Europe.

For many Britons, the 2nd anniversary of Brexit is a rather rude awakening. Brexit has not made them richer – but poorer instead. Recent economic figures are downright humiliating. No country in the G20 performs worse than the UK – apart from the heavily sanctioned Russia.

At the same time, the British pound has crashed. It lost about 20% of its value against the dollar and the Euro. Worse, imports are becoming more expensive and this fuel inflation. While many countries struggle with a devaluation of money, the British have been hit particularly hard. The UK inflation rate was 10.7%.

The economic weakness also affects taxes. The British earned £40 billion less per year than without Brexit. This gives the conservative's ideology of eternal "tax cuts" an entire new meaning.

This money is urgently needed to invest in infrastructure and in the health care system. BoJo's £350 million a week of tax-money saved after leaving the EU turned out to be – yet another – lie. Instead of funding the NHS, as promised by the conservatives, the NHS is in deep crisis.

Even rather small details have become humiliating for the UK. One issue that the London police, for example, had to deal with was that it needed to buy new armored cars "NOT" from a British manufacturer but from Audi. No English company was able to meet the requirements of the tender.

Yet, many Brexit fans had dreamed that their domestic industry would blossom to a whole new size – another lie of the conservatives. Since Brexit came into force in January 2021, the very opposite from what the conservatives promised actually happened.

The past two years have been extremely bitter – even in terms of international politics. Britain's conservatives were forced to come to terms with the fact that there was very little international interest in their economy. No significant trade deal was signed in the last two years.

Instead, the UK was plagued by customs' problems in trade with the EU. In their self-created political hallucinations, UK conservatives had envisioned to conclude a lot of free trade agreements after Brexit. This – as the false propaganda promises went – was designed to grant the British unique advantages.

But in fact, there were substantially new agreements only with rather insignificant trading countries such as, for example, Australia and New Zealand. Worse, these agreements had next to no meaning at all.

These two deals were expected to increase the UK's economic output by a super-negligible 0.1% and 0.03% (!) respectively – in the long term. What the master of the economy – the conservatives – did borders on a bitter joke.

Despite grand Tory propaganda, Brexit has only brought in disadvantages. This is particularly evident in exports. British exports actually should have increased because the pound has fallen so much and British goods are becoming significantly cheaper on world markets. But exports are not getting off the ground. Foremost, because trading with the EU – the UK's most significant trading partner – has become very difficult due to Brexit.

In other words, UK's trading with the EU – its largest trading partner – goes backward. And this is not surprising. After all, the trading area that the UK left, i.e. the EU is only 34km from Britain. Yet since Brexit, British companies have to fill out a jumble of customs' documents if they want to export their goods to Europe.

Despite the Tory claim of "we support small businesses", particularly medium-sized companies are overwhelmed. As a consequence, they either give up completely or set up subsidiaries in the EU to avoid the customs' problems.

In short, Brexit is a disaster for the British. And, it has gotten even worse during the last two years. Today, the majority of the British people regrets Brexit.

There is also a growing awareness in the UK that Brexit was a mistake. In recent surveys, 51% of respondents now say that it was wrong to leave the EU. While 34% still think this decision was right.

However, this change of heart has not had any political consequences so far. The opposition Labor Party prefers to avoid the topic of Brexit in order not to scare away voters. At the same time, the ruling Tories have embarked on a rhetorical rant trying to sell the increasingly unsellable: Brexit.

Recently, PM Rishi Sunak is said to have considered adopting the "Swiss model". Switzerland is not in the EU. Through a special agreement, Switzerland can participate in the internal EU market – it can trade with the EU. And the Swiss can do that without paying significantly to the EU – no membership fees. A similar deal would be perfect for the British – the British conservatives thought.

With a Swiss-style agreement, the UK could continue to save €6.8bn of payments to the EU that the UK used to transfer to the EU. Simultaneously, this would solve their export problems. However, Sunak had to quickly abandon this push. His Tory base did not move with him.

The Swiss model has one disadvantage, at least from the point of view of Brexit fans: they would have to adopt many EU regulations again because the internal market can only work if all participants adhere to the same rules.

Without being represented in the institutions of the EU, Switzerland has virtually no input into shaping EU rules. Switzerland is, therefore, constantly busy adapting its own laws to European decisions. A lot of Brits do not want that.

Conversely, the EU has let it be known that it does not want to re-issue the Swiss model. This is consistent with current EU thinking. The EU could not "sell off" itself, because other countries might also want to leave the EU, in order to save on membership fees. That could mushroom into a fatal consequence for the EU.

When many British are discussing Brexit, they complain mainly about endless customs' forms and empty supermarket shelves. Yet, the real drama takes place elsewhere — in the City of London. Today, British banks are no longer subjected to European supervision and thus lose access to the mainland.

It is not impossible that the British financial sector will shrink by about 30% in the long term. The British can hardly afford such a significant loss in one of their principal export sectors: the UK's financial sector. This is because the income generated from financial services by the City of London are needed to pay for imports into the UK.

In reality, the British have always imported far more than they exported. Worse, this deficit is now continuing to swell. So far, it has not been a serious problem. Britain has borrowed abroad to cover their consumption. The British pound was considered a stable currency. Yet, this may soon be over.

After Brexit and despite the nationalistic rhetoric of the conservatives, it became increasingly noticeable that the UK is in fact a rather small island that has almost no industry. It is rare for a country to deliberately and voluntarily seek to become impoverished. But the British have decided to do just that – perhaps to the Schadenfreude of many.

Conclusion

Just over three years of experiencing Brexit — the United Kingdom leaving the European Union — it appears that Brexit has turned into a debacle. By 2023, there were talks of *Bregret* — the **reg**ret of **Bre**xit. For many, if not most, people inside the UK, in Europe, and even in the European Union, there seemed to be no reason — despite the UK's conservative government's attempt — to celebrate. Partly because of Brexit, the UK's economy had become lame, and households were suffering. Meanwhile, conservative government was preoccupied with itself, its scandals, and a celebration of Brexit that not many wanted to take part in.

Almost in time for their third futile "anniversary" from withdrawing from the EU, the UK's conservatives received further bad news. This time from the International Monetary Fund (IMF). As the Russian war against the Ukraine started to bite in economic term, the IMF's economic forecast for the current year of 2023 was way better for all other major industrialized countries than feared months ago. Even Germany — which was heavily dependent on Russian gas — was getting away with a small level of economic growth.

According to the IMF in early 2023, only the British economy was set not to grow in 2023. Instead, the UK's economy was forecasted to shrink by 0.6%. As a consequence, the UK ranked last in the IMF's assessment – even performing worse than Russia, which – unlike the UK – has been subjected to far-reaching sanctions because of its war of aggression against the Ukraine.

Meanwhile, the UK's conservative treasury secretary – Jeremy Hunt – downplayed the inconvenient forecast. Yet, the IMF figures showed that the UK is not immune to the pressures that almost all developed economies are facing – except these other countries did not have Brexit. Worse, in one long-range forecast, the UK should have grown faster than Germany and Japan. The opposite occurred under the economic management of UK's conservatives.

For the UK's conservative government, however, the IMF's prospects were worse than unflattering. The UK's weak growth came despite the often-rehearsed myth that the conservatism is *good for the economy*. One reason for the UK's downward spiral has been the Brexit-induced shortage of workers. One of the main triggers – among other things – was that Brexit made skilled immigration from the EU to the UK much more difficult, a deterrent, and in some cases, a sheer impossibility.

Beyond all that, the UK leaving the EU has also brought with it other challenges. These too, were inhibiting economic growth – the conservatives' time-honored claim to fame. Among other things like the war in the Ukraine, the UK's economy, businesses, and companies have been suffering from political instability in recent years. Some of which were created by the conservative's zealous drive towards Brexit. Given all that, it was no surprise to see that the UK was – in the years of 2022 and early 2023 – one of the very few large economies that had failed to reach pre-Covid-19 levels in its gross domestic product.

Undeterred by years of political wavering and homemade instability, UK conservatives with BoJo at the helm made sure that on 31st of January 2020 at 11pm – midnight in Brussels – the UK had left the European Union. It was exactly three and a half years after the initial referendum on Brexit. At the end of the same year, participation in the EU's single market and its customs union also ended. Eventually, the UK was freed from *the shackles of the EU*. Yet, the freeing was replaced by a hastily negotiated free trade agreement.

After three years – by the beginning of 2023 – it had become increasingly clear – even to the most hardened pro-Brexit supporter – that there was no substitute for integration into the European market. Today, the conservatives' partners – the so-called business community – complains that the abolition of the free movement of persons has made it more difficult to recruit workers. By 2023, there was a continued and acute shortage of staff everywhere in the UK – from farming to supermarkets to hospitals. In its National Health Service (NHS) for example, things had reached a state of emergency in – no pun intended – the NHS' emergency service.

At the same time, British companies had to deal with overbearing bureaucratic formalities in trade with the EU – even though British conservatives have claimed, for decades, that they would fight red tape and much-hated bureaucracy. Yet, the exact opposite has occurred from what British conservatives were promising when following their neoliberal ideology of freeing the market from administrative burdens.

Worse, the much-acclaimed so-called *golden age* that the Tory government had conjured up after Brexit appeared to be nothing more than another hallucination. Although the government has concluded numerous trade agreements with often rather insignificant scope, these agreements were, more often than not, carbon copies of existing EU treaties. This came from a political party that wanted to exit from the EU – not copying it and continuing EU policies.

Quite apart from all this is the fact that the UK lost trade agreements with other nations as the UK is no longer part of the EU. Since Brexit, the UK is also no longer part of trade agreements negotiated between the EU and other non-EU countries. Some estimate that the UK lost such trade agreements with about seventy countries.

On the upswing, the UK had reached a trade agreement with Australia and New Zeeland. In fact, the UK's post-Brexit agreement with Australia and New Zealand was really a new trade agreement. And it supports British farmers. On the downside, the agreement also expressed the fear of cheap competition from the two – very distant – and somewhat agricultural countries.

Meanwhile, back in the UK, high inflation was somewhat in decline by early 2023. Just a few months earlier, it was still in the double digits – during December 2022. As a response, the Bank of England increased the key interest rate from 3.5% to 4% in February 2023. This was yet another damper for the British economy that the conservatives claim to manage so well.

During the same time, the conservative government's plans to make the UK a leading location in the field of future technologies was designed to come as a compensation for what is known as the *Brexit downturn*. But the recent bankruptcy of the key company – Britishvolt – which wanted to build a new gigafactory for car batteries in the north of England, hardly fitted into the conservative's rosy picture of a golden age after Brexit.

Apart from grand announcements, ideology, and propaganda, the reality of many in the UK is rather different from what the conservatives promised. At a *warm bank* in town called Tupton, for example, people were lining up who do not have enough money for heating. At the warm bank, they can get warmed up.

Meanwhile, the rest of the UK's population is struggling with their own survival. In addition to high inflation, more expenses are added to existing mortgages as a result of interest rate increases. This comes in addition to skyrocketing energy costs. As feared by many experts, the phenomenon of *energy poverty* has started to eat ever deeper into the lower middle class. By early 2023, around one quarter of all British households were affected.

This means that about seven million households do not have enough money to decently heat their often miserably insulated dwellings. It is not surprising that *warm banks*, i.e. public spaces where you can warm up, and *food banks*, where people can get free food, were experiencing a big crowd over the winter of 2022 to 2023.

As so often, Brexit is not solely to blame for the UK's misery. Next to staunchly following the ideology of neoliberalism for decades, spiced up by privatization, union-bashing, the hallucination of the Uber-panacea of the free market and competition, there was also the suicidal economic policy of ultra-short-term prime minister Liz Truss – for a few days – that also contributed to the UK's impoverishment.

Nevertheless, conservative illusions of a *Golden Age* after Brexit were further fueled by the EU exit and mistaken illusion of freeing the UK from *the shackles of the EU.* In a subsequent survey in early 2023, only 9% think that Brexit has had a positive effect on the country.

Pro-Brexit super hardliner like the former economic minister Jacob Rees-Mogg no longer challenged this in 2023. Yet, pro-Brexiteers even wanted to finally abolish all EU regulations that had been incorporated into the UK's national law for almost five decades – 47 years. This is the conservatives' plan even though they failed to explain what benefit this is supposed to have for the economy. It seems increasingly the case as if the fanatical pro-Brexit conservatives are about to leave only *scorched earth* behind.

The UK's pro-Brexiteers work in conjunction with conservative prime minister Rishi Sunak. Because of his free market and free trade neoliberal convictions, some more nationalistic inclined pro-Brexiteers suspect him of being a *disguised remainder* – someone who is secretly harboring thoughts of remaining inside the EU as a preferred policy option.

Yet and this comes in sharp contrast to former conservative prime minister Liz Truss, multi-millionaire Sunak voted to leave the EU in 2016, i.e. he voted *for* Brexit. Since the vote, Sunak has become the fifth Tory Prime Minister contradicting yet another myth, that conservatives seek a stable government.

Not too long into Sunak's premiership, he fired Tory general secretary Nadhim Zahawi – who was one of the richest members of parliament, because Zahawi had "forgotten" (!) to declare a million-dollar fine for tax evasion. By early 2023, an investigation was also underway against deputy prime minister Dominic Raab – a conservative heavyweight – for bullying employees.

This had further damaged Sunak's and the conservatives' reputation. To be compensated for that and to divert attention of the UK's mostly right-wing UK press away from the conservatives, Sunak displayed a tough attitude in dealing with striking civil service employees. Yet, many have given him a *grace period* until local elections in May

2023 – in which the conservative Tories are threatened with a devastating defeat. In the background, Sunak's predecessor Boris Johnson (BoJo) was lurking to re-establish himself.

Funnily, lying and scandal prone BoJo still has many fans utterly convinced that only Boris can prevent an electoral debacle in the 2024 elections. In a survey done in early 2023, the opposition Labor Party was leading the conservative by 23% – implying a landslide victory.

Yet, on the subject of Brexit, Labor leader Keir Starmer was also covering himself so as not to wake sleeping dogs. Many inside the UK's Labor party had voted for Brexit. Wisely and without much of a real chance anyway, Starmer had excluded a return of the UK to the EU or even the single market. Simultaneously, his Labor party has promised the *normalization* of relations to the EU and closer cooperation with the EU. Compared to the conservative's Brexit fiasco, this might indeed be a step forward.

The conservatives have been set on Brexit ever since David Cameron promised a referendum on Britain's membership in the EU on 23rd of January 2013. He vowed that, if the Conservative Party wins the next general election in 2015, there would be a referendum on the UK leaving the EU. Cameron won the election. Yet, the conservative's Brexit politics has created a deeply divided nation. This only deepened with the 2016 Brexit referendum, the *Get Brexit Done!* election of 2019, and the subsequent exit of the UK from the EU on the 31st of January 2020 at 11pm or 23:00 (GMT).

Today, the conservative-induced trenches virtually run between all parts of the country, between city and countryside, between rich and poor, between old and young, and sometimes even between members of the same family. None of these matters to the conservatives. What mattered was winning elections and this is what the conservatives did – for years on end.

Apart from winning elections at the cost of splitting the UK – which was engineered by a rather nationalistic political party – others feared the negative consequences of Brexit for the British economy. In 2023, this fear was no longer a fear. The sentiment was expressed by former Sainsbury's CEO Justin King when noting, *UK supermarkets have been hurt horribly by Brexit.*

Five years before his *"hurt horribly" statement,* in March 2017, negotiations for Brexit were formally initiated by the then conservative prime minister Theresa May. These negotiations were to be completed after two years at the latest. UK conservatives originally wanted to leave the EU on

29th of March 2019. The plan by the conservatives failed.

Unlike the conservative's hallucinations, the Brexit negotiations between the EU Commission and the UK's conservative government barely got off the ground for months. Despite the preliminary promise on a withdrawal agreement in November 2018, there was still a great risk of a "hard Brexit" – an even more total and sharp withdrawal from the EU. Hard Brexit meant a rather disorderly severance of relations with Europe. In the meantime, Theresa May had lost a decisive vote on Brexit in the British parliament in early 2019.

In order to gain time for additional negotiations, Brexit was, subsequently, postponed away from 12th of April 2019 – to a later date. At the EU summit on 21st of March 2019, the 27 EU member states agreed to the UK's wish for a postponement until 12th of April.

Since the British House of Commons had again not approved the withdrawal agreement negotiated with the EU, the UK had to present an alternative before April 12th – or the country would have left the EU on that day without a contract. Because of the further failure of Theresa May, Brexit negotiations were moved to 30th of June 2019. Next, the EU postponed Brexit to 31st of October 2019.

After the resignation of conservative prime minister Theresa May, Boris Johnson or BoJo's new government started to prepare for a *Hard Brexit* – even without an EU agreement. But then, the parliament voted against Brexit without an agreement. Next and at Britain's request, the EU postponed Brexit to 31st of January 2020. After the extremely clear election victory of the conservatives on 12th of December 2019 in BoJo's *Get Brexit Done!* election, Brexit was definitely coming.

In a post-Brexit transition period, the UK remained in the EU's single market and customs union until the end of 2020 to avoid a hard cut for the economy. Meanwhile, Brussels and London had crossed the finish line on 24th of December 2020 with a post-Brexit trade agreement for the transition phase. By 1st of January 2021, the UK was no longer a part of the single market, as well as the EU's customs union. Finally, the UK was free from the shackles of the EU.

Since then, there have been significantly more formalities to be completed for many companies on both sides. Although there will be no customs duties on British goods in the future due to the trade pact, British exporters to the EU will now have to prove that their products were actually and mainly produced in their own country.

For goods from the EU intended for the British market, it must be proven that they actually come from the EU. It is also necessary to provide evidence of compliance with EU rules on food safety and compliance with product standards. For the British service industry, access to the European single market became significantly more difficult with the end of the Brexit transition phase on 31st of December 2020.

In the interim, the economically miniscule but politically significant issue of fishing rights proved to be difficult to solve. European fishermen had to forego a quarter of their fishing quotas. In the meantime – in early 2023 – *Save British Farming* chair Liz Webster said,

the reason that we have food shortages in Britain,
and that we don't have food shortages in Spain
– or anywhere else in the European Union –
is because of Brexit.

With the end of Brexit's transition period, the free movement of people between the EU and the UK also ended. This means that anyone who wants to work and live in the UK from now on must apply for a visa, regulated by a points-based system. However, there is no visa requirement for tourists on shorter trips.

After the UK's complete exit from the EU, the British economy continued to suffer from the dire consequences of Brexit. Today, the UK is not a member of the EU's customs union and the single market. British hopes – as announced by the conservative and turbocharged by Britain's equally conservative press – for a high dividend due to Brexit have not been fulfilled. It was yet another false promise of the conservatives. Worse, Brexit's high goals which the conservatives had advertised Brexit were not achieved – plain and simple. The six most common pro-Brexit promises of the conservatives included:

1. greater autonomy – freeing the UK from the shackles of the EU;
2. less bureaucracy, less administration, and less red tape;
3. less immigration – often mixed with a racist undertone;
4. a better healthcare system where the fees for EU membership were to flow to the NHS;
5. lower taxes; and finally,
6. better bilateral trade agreements.

New trade agreements – such as the one with Australia – were insignificant compared to the losses in trade with the EU. The distance between London and Sydney is 10.500 miles or 17,000km. The distance between Dover and Calais is 27 miles or 43km. The EU has 450 million people. Australia has 26 million. Just in terms of these numbers, post-Brexit UK lost big time as the much-trumpeted Australian trade agreement has not been able to compensate for the loss of access to the EU's market.

By early 2023, it was getting worse considering that less than two-thirds of the foreign trade volume was covered by post-Brexit trade agreements. A trade agreement with the United States, for example, was nowhere in sight as the US prefers to deal with the EU – not with individual states.

According to the nationalistic election propaganda of the conservatives, Brexit was to bring independence free from EU regulations. Further, it was to allow the UK's economy to grow. A look at the data shows that leaving the EU has harmed the UK – the very opposite of the false promises of the conservatives – the supposedly good economic manager.

Still worse, Brexit has deeply divided the country and led to one of the most turbulent political periods in recent British history. It has resulted in two early elections, four resignations of prime ministers – David Cameron, Theresa May, Boris Johnson, and Liz Truss. For the conservatives, it also resulted in numerous historic defeats of the conservative government inside the UK parliament where the conservatives had a clear majority. Surprisingly, neither of the UK's major political parties is any longer questioning the EU exit itself. And both do not – at least not publicly – advocating a return to the EU.

Unlike what was promised by the conservatives, Brexit has in fact led to significantly higher costs of additional administration, more bureaucracy, and increase in red tape, logistics, customs duties, financing, and IT adjustments. At the same time, Brexit has delivered lower sales revenues. Healthcare, transport, hospitality, and agriculture have become the victims of Brexit.

Since Brexit, these industries have been complaining that they lack workers from southern and eastern Europe because of tight immigration rules. In the interim, UK households have become poorer, investments have stagnated, and the trade barriers to the EU's largest sales market have caused the movement of goods to collapse by an estimated 10% to 15%.

Since 2017 – the first year after the Brexit referendum – the importance of the UK as a trading partner, for example, for Germany has been steadily declining – not increased as promised by the conservatives. While still ranked fifth among the most important foreign trade partners in 2017, by 2022, the UK was no longer represented in the top ten of German trade partners.

Thanks to Brexit, the value of the British pound has fallen by about 10% since the EU referendum in June 2016. In other words, the economic master manager – the conservatives – have made the UK not richer but poorer. The decline of the pound made imports more expensive, further fueling inflation. By January 2023, inflation was around ten percent – higher than it has been in the last 40 years.

At the time a recession was also looming while funding costs had risen. A rise in corporate tax from 19% to 25% was scheduled for April 2023. Despite all this, there was no turnaround in sight for the UK's post-Brexit suffering.

Instead of facing the inevitable – that Brexit was a disaster – the conservative prime minister Sunak was blaming the looming recession on Corona, on inflation, and the war in the Ukraine. Worse, according to the Bank of England's forecast, gross domestic product (GDP) is set to shrink steadily for two years between mid-2022 and mid-2024.

Undeterred by the Brexit calamity, UK conservatives – according to their very own and well-crafted myth – continue to present themselves as an independent free trade champion. Surprisingly, Brexit meant the exact opposite. It meant no more free access to the EU's internal market. Inconveniently, this fact is being swept under the carpet.

Worse for the conservative's very own myth, the political dependence of Britain's very powerful financial capital – based in the City of London – on the EU had actually increased and not decreased. Even more problematic for the UK is the fact that the latter – the EU – can now unilaterally decide that British financial market regulation is not equivalent to that of the EU. This would mean that British financial service providers would no longer be able to do business in the EU. In other words, if the UK wants to trade with the EU, it has to follow EU rules but since Brexit, the UK is no longer able to shape those rules.

In terms of access to the EU's services market, the conservative's attempt of squaring the circle failed badly or *horribly* as Sainsbury CEO Justin King would have said. The problem here is that the share of services in British exports is above average. Recently, it was at 44%. Furthermore, the importance of the UK's financial sector can only be maintained by regulations that offer reasonably generous conditions for employees in the service industry to come to the UK or to make them stay in the UK.

However, this counteracts the underlying racist intention of the conservatives, which was, after all, one of the main reasons for the withdrawal from the EU. It was to keep migrant workers away from the UK – especially from Eastern Europe. Various legal disputes will likely to be necessary. This will determine whether the agreed restrictions on the export of services would go too far. This will also determine whether the UK has become unattractive or an impossible location for harvest workers, construction workers, and nurses. Many of those non-British workers had offered – prior to Brexit – their labor through service companies in the UK.

Meanwhile, the majority of Britons are becoming deeply dissatisfied with their country's exit from the EU. Interestingly, by early 2023, and 70,000 people strong from a north-eastern town of Boston was the last place in the UK where the majority of people still thought that leaving the EU was a good idea.

Beautiful half-timbered houses, a large Gothic church in the city center, a hospital with good job opportunities, all in bright sunshine. If one believed the public relations' film of the University of Lincoln, one would get the impression of an idyllic summer paradise.

But if you spend time looking closer at the town, you will find out rather quickly what else Boston stands for. Only about fifteen years ago, the place was considered to be the city where most people were overweight. In 2016, Boston had the highest murder rate in England and Wales – even ahead of London. In the same year, 76% of voters in Boston supported Brexit, more than anywhere else in the UK.

It seems as if even for the town of Boston, more and more people are doubting whether they made the right decision when voting for Brexit. Elsewhere in the UK, the majority of people in Scotland, England, and Wales now consider that leaving the EU was wrong.

Yet today, Boston still remains somewhat of an exception when it comes to the realization that Brexit has some very serious and largely negative consequence for the UK and for Boston. By early 2023, in Boston, a whopping 41% of the local respondents continue to believe that leaving the EU was the right decision. Meanwhile, 37% of Bostoners were against Brexit in early 2023. There were several reasons as to why the mood against the European Union particularly was strong in Boston.

If one wanted to understand the Brexit-friendly atmosphere, one would have to take a closer look at the economic situation of the counties of Lincolnshire and Boston. Almost a third of the jobs in the city come from agriculture. The region around Boston is considered the breadbasket of Great Britain – 30% of all British vegetables come from there, and 18% of poultry production is also located there.

A decisive turning point in the history of Boston was the year 2004, when ten new states joined the EU. In the following years, many people from Portugal, Poland, and the Baltic states came to Boston's area to work in agriculture. In 2011, Boston was the place in the UK that had the highest percentage of migrants from Eastern Europe. In just seven years, the share had increased almost six fold.

Since then, the mood in Boston had become correspondingly hostile. A local politician from the Brexit party Ukip said in 2016, *they come here and the first thing they do is apply for a social housing. And then other social benefits*. Perhaps this might be a slight misrepresentation of the British welfare state that has been significantly reduced – if not destroyed – since the arrival of Thatcher in the 1980s, and the relentless drive to convert Hayek's ideology of neoliberalism into actual reality.

But there is a second version of the same story. This sounds rather different from a place that supposedly suffers from over-alienation. *The immigrants saved the city*, said another local in 2015. In reality, small business owners had become dependent on cheap labor from abroad, especially in agriculture. Many locals no longer wanted those jobs.

Between 2012 and 2019, per capita income in Lincolnshire increased from £19,630 to almost £23,900 pounds – from $23,700 to $28,850. But the truth is also that the region belongs to the lower half of Great Britain.

In fact, the unemployment rate in the city was more often below than above the national average. *We came here for a better life. We work hard, we pay taxes, we shop*, a Polish Boston resident said. It is a rather common story. Yet, the man also said, *they* [the British] *don't want to work at all. They only apply for social security benefits.*

Besides all this, Britain's conservative government claimed to have won a victory by listing the concessions that the EU was supposed to have made elsewhere. This is contrasted with the so-called *level playing field* – the enforcement of common rules and standards.

However, this turns the reality of the UK-EU conflict upside down. The EU limits the UK market access because Britain's conservatives have convinced themselves that they can have economic relations with the EU without the associated legal system. The UK's *level playing field*, for example, includes the UK's withdrawal from social and labor law.

In particular, the European Court of Justice continued to be *a red flag* to hard-core conservative Brexiteers. This was used by the then British Prime Minister Boris Johnson to boosts his negotiating skills because the court no longer plays a role in disputes – post-Brexit. Beyond that, the fact that there is no longer a right to vote in EU institutions for the UK was not the reason but is a consequence of leaving the EU.

In the end, the UK has not won anything from the EU despite the multiple claims by British conservatives. Rather, British capitalism has lost access to an important marketplace – the EU. The exceptional idiocy of power-hungry British conservatism engineered Brexit for the party's and a few Tory prime ministers. In short, it was done for their own benefit rather than for the UK's benefit.

Simultaneously, the Tories claimed to work for the betterment of the UK. This obscures to the extent to which British conservatives themselves are part of a long-lasting political crisis of keeping capitalism alive. By doing that, it caused an unimaginable amount of Brexit misery. This misery continued for a long time after Brexit. And it did this whether a substantial number of British people regret Brexit or not – the rise of *Bregret*.

Sources:

Brexiting Through the Media
Originally published on: 11th August, 2016
https://www.counterpunch.org/2016/08/11/brexiting-through-the-media/

Brexit, History & Ballot Choice
Originally published on: 1st of February 2020
https://countercurrents.org/2020/02/brexit-history-ballot-choice/

How Brexit Won
Originally published on: 12th February, 2021
https://www.counterpunch.org/2021/02/12/how-brexit-won/

Post-Brexit Truck Driving – a Driver's Report
Originally published on: 12th February 2021
https://countercurrents.org/2021/02/post-brexit-truck-driving-a-drivers-report/

The Dark Money and Dirty Politics of Brexit
Originally published on: 5th February, 2021
https://www.counterpunch.org/2021/02/05/the-dark-money-and-dirty-politics-of-brexit/

Brexit Anxieties
Originally published on: 7th January, 2021
https://www.counterpunch.org/2021/01/07/brexit-anxieties/

Brexit Bites Back
Originally published on: 12th December, 2022
https://www.counterpunch.org/2022/12/12/brexit-bites-back/

The Schadenfreude of Brexit
Originally published on: 2nd February 2023
https://countercurrents.org/2023/02/the-schadenfreude-of-brexit/